Makers of Modern Science

ROBERT OPPENHEIMER
DARK PRINCE

Jack Rummel

Facts On File

New York • Oxford

With love to Ann Lowe

ROBERT OPPENHEIMER: DARK PRINCE

Copyright © 1992 by Jack Rummel

All rights reserved. No part of this book may be reproduced or utilized in any form or by any means, electronic or mechanical, including photocopying, recording, or by any information storage or retrieval systems, without permission in writing from the publisher. For information contact:

Facts On File, Inc.
460 Park Avenue South
New York NY 10016
USA

Facts On File Limited
Collins Street
Oxford OX4 1XJ
United Kingdom

Library of Congress Cataloging-in-Publication Data
Rummel, Jack
Robert Oppenheimer: dark prince / Jack Rummel.
    p. cm. — (Makers of modern science)
Includes bibliographical references and index.
ISBN 0-8160-2598-3
1. Oppenheimer, J. Robert, 1904–1967—Juvenile literature. 2. Atomic bomb—United States—History—Juvenile literature. 3. Physicists—United States—Biography—Juvenile literature.
I. Title. II. Series.
QC16.062R85 1992
623.4'5199'092—dc20   91-17659

A British CIP catalogue record for this book is available from the British Library.

Facts On File books are available at special discounts when purchased in bulk quantities for businesses, associations, institutions or sales promotions. Please call our Special Sales Department in New York at 212/683-2244 (dial 800/322-8755 except in NY, AK, or HI) or in Oxford at 865/728399.

Text design by Ron Monteleone
Jacket design by Catherine Hyman
Composition by Facts On File, Inc.
Manufactured by the R. R. Donnelley & Sons
Printed in the United States of America

10 9 8 7 6 5 4 3 2 1

This book is printed on acid-free paper.

CONTENTS

ACKNOWLEDGMENTS

With special thanks to:

Roger A. Meade, archivist, Los Alamos National Laboratory
Mollie G. Rodriguez, Los Alamos National Laboratory
Theresa A. Strottman, archivist, Los Alamos Historical Museum
Los Alamos National Laboratory
The New York Public Library
Remmel Nunn
Helen Flynn
Nicole Bowen

1

BRIGHTER THAN A THOUSAND SUNS

The three sedans rolled slowly down a muddy backcountry road and came to a halt in front of a solitary wooden building set at the edge of a deep canyon. Two men in civilian clothes got out of the middle car and sprinted into the building. Six more men, three each in the front and back automobiles, loitered around the other car. All six were dressed in military uniforms, and several carried holstered pistols. Another man, Philip Morrison, who worked as a physicist at this unlikely place, remained in the back seat of the middle sedan. Afflicted by polio as a child, Morrison was unable to help the other civilians with their task; instead he had been given the honor of riding shotgun with an extraordinarily precious load of cargo.

The building in front of which this miniconvoy stopped was not well made. It had the cheap, almost shanty look of a place that had been thrown together quickly. In typical army fashion, it had been given a bland and nondescript name, Omega site.

Omega constituted one part of a complex of barracks and halls that had been hastily constructed during the previous two years on a sprawling flat-topped mesa in northern New Mexico. This place was called Los Alamos, a Spanish word that means the cottonwood trees. Even though it had a nice ring, the name was not apt. Few cottonwoods grew at Los Alamos's 8,000-foot altitude; instead an immense forest of ponderosa pine and Douglas fir, highlighted here and there with bright green swatches of aspen, encircled the mesa. The view of the surrounding mountains was spectacular, and from some spots one could see beyond the mountains and onto the vast desert that stretched to the edge of the horizon.

Formerly the home of a strict, disciplinarian boys' school, Los Alamos was isolated from the outside, which was why the site had been chose by the army to house laboratories for its most secret project. Only a few people beyond the gates knew of Los Alamos's existence. Even the local people, who occasionally picked up the unannounced Sunday afternoon concerts of classical music broadcast on the laboratory's private radio station, knew only that "the government" was holding some kind of "war work" out in the mountains at the old boys' school.

War work was not uncommon in July 1945. In a sense, the entire country was engaged in war work. Three and a half years into its struggle with the Axis powers of Germany and Japan, the government and people of the United States had pushed their economy into high gear, producing equipment of war for the nation and its allies. The little enterprise at Los Alamos scarcely raised an eyebrow amid the bustle. Most people in northern New Mexico thought of Los Alamos, if they knew of it at all, as just another sleepy army post that was the site of some kind of obscure and relatively unimportant ordnance activity, something along the line of explosives research or the study of bazookas.

Within minutes, the two civilians emerged from the rickety building pulling a dolly loaded with a single small crate. Another man carried an object about the size of a car battery that seemed to be held together by a series of protruding bolts. A handle had been affixed to the awkward-looking contraption so that it could be carried without actually having to heft it next to the body. Both the box and the batterylike object, though small, were evidently heavy, because the men strained to load them into the car. Carefully they worked the crate and the other object into the back seat of the middle sedan next to Philip Morrison. When everything had been secured, the little caravan began to wend its way down the mountain road toward Santa Fe.

They passed unnoticed through Santa Fe and turned south, traveling through Albuquerque and beyond, following the Rio Grande until they came to the hamlet of San Antonio. There they turned off the main road and passed onto another dusty back road that led out to a place of utter desolation called the Jornada del Muerto, known in English as the Journey of Death.

Running almost 60 miles north and south and 40 miles east to west, the Jornada del Muerto is a waterless plain of volcanic rock and sand infested with rattlesnakes, scorpions and tarantulas. During the summer months temperatures on the Jornada often top 100°F. The Spanish had given this place its ominous name in the 17th century, and even in 1945 a trek across it was not something that most people took lightly.

The men in the three cars traveled for almost two hours more on increasingly poor roads that took them farther into the heart of the sweeping desert plain, until at last the road simply quit at an adobe ranch house. This was the McDonald ranch, a spread of several thousand acres only recently acquired by the U.S. government.

Corral at the McDonald ranch, looking across the Jornada del Muerto.
(Los Alamos National Laboratory)

Here the couriers were met by an excited group of scientists and military men, and their cargo was hastily unloaded.

After the crates had been carried to the ranch house, Philip Morrison paused to examine the setup inside. Cluttered with electrical wires and cables that linked an array of scientific equipment, the living room looked like a cross between the bridge of a spaceship and the last hideout of Billy the Kid. Lab-coated technicians uncrated the prizes from Los Alamos and spread them out on a table covered with plain brown wrapping paper. Five objects were pulled from the two containers: one small metal sphere and four other half-spheres that were shaped like peaches with their pits removed. The smallest object, the single complete sphere, bore an astonishing resemblance to a miniature golf ball. It was about as large as a marble, and like the surface of a golf ball, its surface was dimpled. The ball, in the language of Los Alamos, was "hot," that is, it was composed of material that emitted particles from its atomic structure. This process of emission is called radioactivity.

The ball was made of the metallic elements beryllium and polonium. The polonium was by far the more radioactive of the two substances. Mainly it emits alpha rays, proton-neutron clusters that are continuously ejected from the polonium's unstable atomic nuclei. In its pure state polonium looks somewhat like the kryptonite of a Superman comic book. A blue glow envelopes it and seems to nestle it within a supernatural shield; the hundreds of thousands of neutrons per second that are thrown out of the heart of the polonium atom cause this glow.

Next to the polonium-beryllium sphere lay two dazzling hemispheres that had been plated with nickel and gold. These hemispheres were each made of pure plutonium that had been covered on the curved sides with nickel plating and on the flat surface with a thin sheet of solid gold. Designed to fit together to form a single ball, each of these hemispheres had a small circular notch gouged out of its center. In this pocket the technicians planned to insert the polonium-beryllium golf ball, called the initiator, as they joined the two plutonium hemispheres together. In turn, the plutonium ball would be enclosed in the last of the objects brought from Los Alamos—two rather dull-looking, plum-colored hemispheres made of uranium. Completely assembled, these three balls formed a single ball that weighed approximately 80 pounds and was about the size of a cantaloupe. The entire piece formed the core of the first atomic bomb.

Among the hundred-odd men and women working at the McDonald ranch that Thursday afternoon, July 12, 1945, one in particular seemed to be everywhere at once. His name was Robert Oppenheimer, and he was the director of the Los Alamos Laboratory. At 41, Oppenheimer had reached the prime of his career as a theoretical physicist. At Los Alamos he had assembled a team composed of many of the finest physicists in the world, men and women who in the years before World War II had completely changed humankind's understanding of the structure of the atom. For two years, Oppenheimer had been responsible for supervising this brainy crew, a group that the military commander of the bomb project had dubbed "the biggest collection of eggheads ever."

Before the technicians began to assemble the core of the bomb, an odd ceremony occurred in the living room of the McDonald ranch house. Robert Bacher, one of Oppenheimer's assistants presented to General Thomas Farrell of the U.S. Army an invoice officially acknowledging that the lab had handed over the core of the bomb to the army. Several of the scientists protested that this invoice was an unnecessary waste of time, but Bacher insisted, and Farrell willingly signed the document. The core of the bomb was extraordinarily valuable. At that point in the project, the cantaloupe-sized, triple-layered ball was only one of three atomic cores to be manufactured by a vast network of secret government factories. The total cost of production to that date was $2 billion, easily making the core on the table of the McDonald ranch several hundred times more valuable than an equal weight in diamonds. This great cost made Bacher nervous, and he wanted to be sure that the lab had something on paper showing it had successfully completed its task.

Before he signed the document, General Farrell picked up the glittering plutonium sphere. He held it in his hand for a moment then quickly put it down. He had meant only to feel its weight (Farrell had joked that he wanted to see if the army was getting its money's worth). But rather than being impressed by the heft of the sphere, Farrell was unnerved by the heat of the plutonium. It had the feel, one of those present that day said, "of a live rabbit."

By the day the bomb core arrived at the McDonald ranch, the pressure and fast pace of the bomb project had taken its toll on Robert Oppenheimer's health and emotional well-being. Although Oppenheimer stood six feet tall, he now weighed only 114 pounds. Tense and preoccupied, he constantly scurried from one part of the McDonald ranch to another, conducting last-minute checks to satisfy himself that everything worked as it should. Many final details still had to be resolved before he could be sure that the weapon would actually explode properly, and Oppenheimer, a nervous man in even the most peaceful of times, had become so agitated that others in the project had begun to worry for him.

With Oppenheimer hovering over them, the assembly team worked through most of the night putting the core together. On Friday afternoon, coincidentally Friday the 13th, the rest of the bomb arrived from Los Alamos. It was large, five feet in diameter, bigger than most conventional bombs, although it was not as big as the air force's monster 10,000-pound blockbusters. It was encased in a riveted steel jacket and ensnared in wires that led to timers attached to the bomb's explosive mechanisms. To leave room for the implantation of the radioactive core at the center of the bomb, a few explosive pieces had been set aside. That night in preparation for final assembly, Oppenheimer ordered workers to truck the bomb and the core to the test firing site. The next morning, after only a few hours' sleep, exhausted technicians completed assembly of the core and winched the bomb to the top of a 100-foot tower.

Robert Oppenheimer named the site of this hoped-for, first-ever nuclear explosion Trinity after a sonnet by the English poet John Donne, which reads in part:

Batter my heart, three-personed God; for you
As yet but knock, breathe, shine and seek to mend;
That I may rise, and stand, o'erthrow me, and bend
Your force, to break, blow, burn, and make me new.

Oppenheimer, who was at least as much a philosopher as a scientist, believed that Donne's poem set the proper tone for the experiment at Trinity. If everything worked as planned, on Monday morning before dawn, July 16, 1945, the team of physicists from Los Alamos would unleash an awesome force at Trinity site. As a result of this force, in ways both anticipated and unexpected, the world would become a different place than it had been before.

This power, the result of the energy generated by splitting the atom, represented an enormous technological advance, but one whose immediate purpose was to kill rather than to make life better for humanity. Everyone involved in the project knew that the weapon they had designed was capable, if it worked properly, of killing many thousands of people in a single blast. The army hoped that the bomb would be such an awesome weapon of destruction that the Japanese (in July 1945 the sole remaining enemy of the United States) would immediately surrender rather than risk being annihilated by repeated attacks. Yet, Oppenheimer believed that another, more hopeful outcome might result from unlocking the secret of the atom: The appearance of the atomic bomb signaled a startlingly new era for humankind. The bomb, Oppenheimer speculated, just might, for the first time, make the idea of war impossible because it would introduce such a terrifying weapon into warfare that political leaders would be afraid to use it lest they risk total destruction of their own countries. If the bomb produced a stalemate between competing nations, then it was possible that out of this stalemate humans would have to learn how to negotiate settlements rather than win them on the battlefield.

This was Oppenheimer's hope. However, such speculation was far from his mind during the weekend of July 14 and 15. On Saturday the 14th, a mock-up of the Trinity bomb—minus the lethal plutonium core—was test fired in one of the canyons near Los Alamos. Results of the test apparently showed that the firing had been a failure. This news, telephoned to Oppenheimer by the respected physicist Hans Bethe, threw a gloom over those working at Trinity site. Oppenheimer ordered Bethe to recheck the mathematical calculations upon which the test firing was based, a long and tedious process that kept Bethe up all night.

On Sunday morning Bethe called with partially good news. Because of a math error, the instrument measuring the test firing was unable to tell if the explosives test had been a failure or a success. Thus it was possible that the test *could have been* a success, although no one would know that for sure until the fully assembled bomb was fired at Trinity.

News of the possible failure of the test bomb threw Robert Oppenheimer into an even more agitated state. Scores of government and army officials had been invited to witness the firing of the bomb at Trinity site. Oppenheimer tensely broke this latest, discouraging information to them. Then he worked ceaselessly through the day, chain-smoking cigarettes and coughing violently. He went to bed late and slept only a few fitful hours. Meanwhile, someone improvised a poem that circulated around the ranch that cool summer night:

> From this crude lab has spawned a dud.
> Their necks to Truman's axe uncurled,
> Lo, the embattled savants stood
> And fired a flop heard around the world.

Oppenheimer had ample reason to be nervous. Besides the uncertainty of success of the bomb itself, the weather at Trinity site played an important role in the decision of whether or not the bomb should be fired. The scientists involved in the project knew that the bomb would suck up huge amounts of dirt and debris from the desert floor and send this material high into the atmosphere. This residue, called fallout, would become contaminated by the radioactivity of the bomb, the uranium and plutonium that caused the explosion. If the wind were strong and blowing the wrong way, this fallout could be carried hundreds of miles across the desert, dropping on innocent civilians in towns and cities along the way. Because of these concerns, the project meteorologist established a set of weather guidelines for the test firing: The bomb would be exploded only if the wind was blowing in a direction that would carry the fallout away from cities and towns and if there was no chance of rain (which could dump large amounts of the fallout in a small area) immediately after the test.

The army had taken few precautions to cover themselves in the event of a mistake in the test. Groups of intelligence officers and enlisted men had secretly been stationed in a number of towns and cities around the test site. They would help organize evacuations of these places in the event of an emergency. However, only a relatively small number of men had been assigned this role, and there probably weren't enough of them to do their job properly. The army hoped for a picture-perfect bomb firing; they would have to improvise to deal with catastrophe.

To complicate Oppenheimer's task even more, in the hours just before the explosion a rumor had spread among the enlisted men and technicians at Trinity site that the bomb might set the Earth's atmosphere on fire, perhaps incinerating all of New Mexico or even the whole surface of the Earth itself. Senior scientists were dispatched to reassure the men. Within a few hours, an uneasy calm was restored. But, ironically, the rumor had originated with the senior scientists themselves. Not even those scientists most involved with the building of the bomb could predict exactly what would happen when the device exploded. The experiment at Trinity was a step into the unknown.

The hour of the test had been set for four o'clock in the morning, a time chosen because most of the civilian population in the surrounding area would be asleep (and thus presumably unaware of what had happened out in the Jornada del Muerto) and because the blast could be best observed by scientists at night.

At two in the morning, Oppenheimer was awakened for a meeting with General Leslie Groves, the national director of the project to build the bomb, and Jack Hubbard, the army's meteorologist. A fierce desert storm had blown over the Jornada during the night; heavy rain pelted the command bunker that was dug into the ground just a little less than two miles from the Trinity tower, atop which the bomb now sat. No one wanted to cancel the explosion. Only the most dire weather conditions, such as a strong wind blowing toward Albuquerque or a rainstorm, could have forced a postponement.

Because of the likelihood of continuing rain, Jack Hubbard told Oppenheimer and Groves that the bomb could not be exploded at four o'clock as planned. If the test was to be conducted at all, it would have to be later, between five and six in the morning. Oppenheimer and Groves chose five-thirty as the new hour for the detonation and waited nervously at the command center bunker.

By four o'clock the rain had almost completely stopped and the wind moved around to the southwest, away from major population centers. The team of soldiers and scientists, numbering in the hundreds, moved out to their stations to prepare the instruments that would monitor the test. Twenty miles away, on a rise in the desert floor called Compania Hill, visiting dignitaries, military men and scientists were issued welder's glasses and warned to view the explosion through them to protect their eyes. The brilliance of the blast, they were told, would be brighter than the sun. Watching the blast with the naked eye might result in at least temporary blindness.

At five o'clock, everyone was in place. The final 30 minutes seemed to last an eternity. As the last seconds wound down, Robert Oppenheimer grew tenser and seemed to sag under the effort he had expended on behalf of this enormous scientific endeavor. According to one observer, "He scarcely breathed," and "held on to a post to steady himself."

The flash of the blast startled everyone who saw it. Enrico Fermi, the respected Italian physicist who had worked on the project with Oppenheimer, viewed the explosion from Compania Hill. "Although I did not look directly toward the object, I had the impression that suddenly the countryside became brighter than in full daylight . . . After a few seconds the rising flames lost their brightness and appeared as a huge mushroom that rose rapidly beyond the clouds."

William Laurence, a reporter for the *New York Times* and the only journalist allowed to view the test, wrote a less restrained impression in his journal. "It was like the grand finale of a mighty symphony of the elements, fascinating and terrifying, uplifting and crushing, ominous, devastating, full of great promise and great foreboding."

To Philip Morrison, 10 miles away, the blast seemed like "the desert sun in the midst of night."

An army officer put it more simply. "The longhairs [the scientists] have let it get away from them," he said as the shock wave from the blast ripped across the desert.

In Los Alamos, 155 miles away, the wife of one of the scientists who monitored the test at Trinity site, walked to the edge of a mesa and waited quietly in the darkness. "Then it came," she wrote later.

"The blinding light like no other light one had ever seen. The trees, illuminated, leaping out. The mountains flashing into life. Later, the long, low rumble."

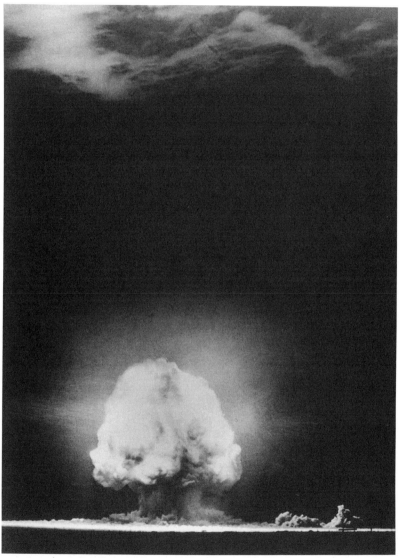

Detonation of the first atomic weapon, Trinity site, July 16, 1945.
(Los Alamos National Laboratory)

Back in the desert at Trinity, Robert Oppenheimer stumbled out of the command bunker to look at the fiery colossus he had done so much to unleash. Exhausted and stunned, he watched the poisonous cloud grow to gigantic size, then fade away into the twilight of dawn. As he observed this, a verse from the Hindu religious poem the *Bhagavad Gita* sprang to mind. In this verse the god Vishnu tries to persuade a prince to perform his duty, even though this duty would destroy the world.

> *If the radiance of a thousand suns*
> *Were to burst at once into the sky,*
> *That would be like the splendor of the Mighty One*
> *. . . . .*
> *I am become Death*
> *The destroyer of worlds.*

At that moment, Robert Oppenheimer, proud of his achievement, yet wary of it, too, felt the burden of that ancient Hindu prince. He had created the "radiance of a thousand suns" and in doing so, it was possible that he had also become a "destroyer of worlds." For as long as he lived, the burden of this moment would remain with him.

CHAPTER 1 NOTES

p. 10   "Although I did not look directly . . ." Manhattan Engineering District Records 319.1, National Archives.

p. 10   "It was like the grand finale . . ." *Los Alamos 1943–1945: The Beginning of an Era*, Los Alamos National Laboratory Reprint 79-78, p. 53.

pp. 10–11   "Then it came . . ." *Los Alamos 1943–1945: The Beginning of an Era*, Los Alamos National Laboratory Reprint 79-78, p. 54.

2

"ASK ME A QUESTION AND I WILL ANSWER YOU IN GREEK"

Turn-of-the-century New York, where Robert Oppenheimer was born on April 22, 1904, was the economic and scientific capital of the United States, and it offered Oppenheimer the advantage of being in the midst of the newest discoveries in science and the application of these discoveries to the machines of technology. For instance, Thomas Edison, the Wizard of Menlo Park, whose laboratories gave to the world the phonograph, the light bulb and electrical power generators, lived and worked only 60 miles away. Furthermore, three excellent universities were located in the city or within a quick train commute from the city.

Changes in technology spurred changes in the way people lived, and New York around 1900 was a city gripped by change. The old ways of the 19th century, characterized by a slow pace of life, horse-drawn transportation, steam-driven industries and old-fashioned, traditional relationships between men and women, were slowly passing from the scene. New scientific discoveries and technological inventions had begun to transform the pace of the city, but the shape of things to come was far from clear.

Turn-of-the-century New York was a bustling place, yet the world of its inhabitants was startlingly different from that of today. Many of the technological conveniences now taken for granted either did not exist or were only in the early stages of development then. For instance, the first electrical power plant ever built was constructed in 1882 in New York by Thomas Edison. Inspired by recent discoveries about electricity by physicists such as Michael Faraday and James Maxwell, Edison's steam-powered, 110-volt generators created electricity for 400 customers in lower Manhattan who had replaced their gas lights with Edison's newly invented carbon filament light bulbs.

Telephones also were a recent addition to the world into which Robert Oppenheimer was born. By 1904 approximately 20,000 households in New York City had phones. The first long distance telephone line linking New York to Chicago had been installed in 1897, only seven years before Oppenheimer's birth.

The automobile, too, was a recent invention. Emile Levassor made the first prototype car in 1891 in Paris. By 1899, 30 American automobile companies had manufactured just 2,500 cars. Before 1904, a mere handful of automobiles chugged through the city's streets, and most people still got from one place to another the old-fashioned way—by walking or in horse-drawn carriages. As a result, there was little air pollution, although the streets smelled terribly of horse manure.

Even the way buildings were constructed changed with new breakthroughs in science and technology. Before 1900, the tallest buildings in Manhattan were 11 stories high. Architects and builders could not make them any higher because steel girders that would support higher buildings had not been perfected. In 1913, proud New Yorkers witnessed the building of the first true skyscraper in New York, the Woolworth Building, which contained over 40 stories and rose more than 450 feet in the air.

In the field of aviation, the Wright Brothers flew the first airplane in 1907, three years before Oppenheimer was born. And the radio only really began to be used after 1909, when a performance of the great Italian tenor Enrico Caruso was broadcast from the roof of the Metropolitan Opera House in New York City and received 30 miles away in Newark, New Jersey, by Lee De Forest, the engineer who was instrumental in perfecting radio broadcast.

This was Robert Oppenheimer's world. It was dynamic, in flux and powered by technological invention and scientific discovery. Technology and science were seen as the saviors of humankind, the tools many people believed would finally liberate them from their days of never-ending toil.

Julius Oppenheimer, Robert's father, was a man very much of the Old World of the 19th century. Julius had come to New York from Germany at age 17 in 1888 and had worked his way up the ladder of success in the United States. Young and poor when he arrived and possessing few job skills, he could speak little English and was unfamiliar with American habits. Yet he was fortunate to have members of his family already in the United States, from whom he got a job and learned how to prosper in his adopted country.

Two of his older cousins had come to New York about a dozen years before Julius's arrival. They had set up a small business importing cloth that was used to make suits and dresses to be sold ready-made in what was then a rapidly growing type of enterprise—the downtown department store. Before long, their business had grown large enough so that they could offer a job to Julius.

Like many other immigrants, the Oppenheimer family came to America to escape religious persecution and seek its fortune. Because they were Jews, the Oppenheimers undoubtably were aware of and resented the prejudice and restrictions placed against them in Europe. Jews were barred from studying in certain schools and discouraged from entering many professions in a number of European countries. And even though it was possible for Jews to become rich and respectable in Europe during the 19th century, most of them were not wealthy and few ever really felt welcome in European society.

The United States, on the other hand, seemed to offer a sanctuary where Jews and others could prosper, live in peace with their fellow citizens and freely practice their religion without fear of persecution. However, in spite of its relative tolerance of minorities, the United States was far from an idyllic nation for new immigrants. It, too, had its anti-Semites (people who were prejudiced against Jews) and its clubs and universities that were reluctant to admit Jews into their ranks. Yet, compared to Europe, the United States was a haven. Soon the newly arriving Jews had a name for their adopted country: They called it the "Golden Land."

Because religion and government were officially separated in the United States, a climate of tolerance and openness had been created that, coupled with a booming economy, offered a chance of success to the industrious and lucky. Even though few immigrants became wealthy during their lifetimes, most could at least comfort themselves with the knowledge that they had been able to provide a better life for their children in America than would have been available in Europe.

Robert Oppenheimer's mother, Ella, had already benefited from this atmosphere of freedom. Ella also was Jewish and came from a family that had lived in New York for several generations. Her family, the Friedmans, prospered in the United States and was well established by the time Ella met Julius Oppenheimer in 1902. This prosperity allowed Ella the leisure to study painting not only in New York but also in Paris. By the time she met Julius Oppenheimer, Ella Friedman had begun to make a name for herself as a painter and art teacher in her own studio in Manhattan.

The couple married in 1903. Robert, their first child, was born the following year. Robert's full name was J. Robert Oppenheimer, the initial J. apparently being an abbreviation of Julius, his father's name. Young Robert either did not like the name Julius or found the initial J. awkward, because throughout his life he used his full name only when signing documents. To everyone else he was known simply as Robert, or later, to his close friends and students, as Oppie.

Several years after Robert's birth, a second boy, Frank, was born to the Oppenheimers. By this time, Julius Oppenheimer's fortune had risen with the burgeoning family business, and the Oppenheimers were able to settle down to a quiet life in a large apartment on fashionable Riverside Drive, located in Manhattan's Upper West Side. After her marriage, Ella no longer had time to pursue painting as a career, so she had given up her studio. From then on, she devoted herself to raising her children and painted occasionally as a hobby. Ella may have resented having to give up painting, but because of the strict customs of the time, she kept these resentments to herself. Her role in turn-of-the-century New York was to care for her family, and the pressure on her to conform to this role was enormous.

Julius and Ella Oppenheimer appeared to get along well, even though their relationship occasionally seemed strained and distant. They kept a formal and proper home staffed with a cook, servants and a chauffeur. In keeping with the Old-World, European atmosphere of their household, meals were formal and disciplined affairs. Both adults and children were expected to be

Julius Oppenheimer holding his son Robert, about 1906.
(J. Robert Oppenheimer Memorial Committee)

properly dressed for meals, either in suits and ties for the men and boys or full-length dresses for the women and girls. Robert also had to be properly dressed for activities outside the home, and if he was going more than a few blocks, he was driven by a chauffeur in the family's motorcar.

Every summer the Oppenheimers, like other wealthy and fashionable New Yorkers, moved their family to an estate in the countryside on Long Island. The family spent the whole summer there in the clean air and near the cooling waters of the ocean. The Oppenheimers' summer home was located near the town of Bay Shore on the southern side of Long Island near the Atlantic Ocean. During the weekdays, Robert spent long hours learning to read or at play with his brother Frank. On the weekends, when Julius Oppenheimer came out to rest from his work in the city, Robert tagged along with his father to the beach or sailed with his father, aunts and uncles on the family sailboat. It was a happy time for him, but it was also a time during which he felt a quiet undercurrent of sadness in his family. A family friend, Paul Horgan, described the Oppenheimers this way:

> She [Ella Oppenheimer] was a very delicate person . . . highly attenuated emotionally . . . but a mournful person. Mr. Oppenheimer was . . . desperately amiable, anxious to be agreeable, and I think essentially a very kind man . . . The household was run with luxury but simplicity at the same time. . . . [Nonetheless] there was a melancholy tone.

From early in his life, Robert displayed an interest in science, a desire to understand and explain how the events in the physical world around him behaved. When he was five, his parents took him and his brother Frank back to Germany to visit his grandfather, Benjamin, who had remained in Europe after Julius Oppenheimer immigrated to the United States. His grandfather gave Robert a gift of a collection of minerals. The chiseled and glittering stones immediately captivated the boy. After he returned to the United States, he became a devoted amateur mineralogist, often touring the countryside during weekends in search of new samples to add to his collection. His fascination with geology and mineralogy became so strong that by his 11th birthday he had become an elected member of the New York Mineralogical Club. His first scientific paper was a report about minerals that he read to the club when he was 12.

Robert also developed a keen interest in literature. When he was not immersed in his study of crystals and minerals, he read voraciously. He also began to write dreamy philosophical poems.

The school Robert had begun to attend, the New York School for Ethical Culture, encouraged his interests in science, literature and philosophy. He was enrolled at the School for Ethical Culture for almost the whole period of his precollege studies—from second grade until he graduated from high school.

The school was run by the philosopher and educator Felix Adler. Adler, like Oppenheimer's father a first-generation American, fervently believed that humans and the society formed by them could be made more perfect, more rational if the members of that society understood and acted on what he called the "supremacy of moral law." At all levels, the school curriculum stressed the responsibility of the individual to the larger society and emphasized the learning of languages, literature, art, science and, most of all, ethics. "Moral law" was taught, beginning with small children, through study and discussion of fairy tales and folklore, and later for older children by study of history, the Old and New Testament and classics of Western literature such as *The Odyssey*. Adler hoped that by acquainting his students with these disciplines he would "awaken the sentiment of humanity, or understanding sympathy with human nature in its various guises."

To achieve this end, many classic works from the Greek and Roman world were taught to the older students in the original languages of these texts. In this way, Robert Oppenheimer first tasted the thrill of language, developed a liking for philosophical writing and sensed the mystery of the world that lay outside his comfortable apartment on Riverside Drive.

Robert flourished at the School for Ethical Culture. His grades were excellent—nearly all A's. By the time he was 11, he bragged to one of his cousins, "Ask me a question and I will answer you in Greek."

Even though Robert excelled in his studies, he began to have difficulties making friends. He wasn't exactly a shy child, but he had become somewhat aloof, a characteristic he had learned perhaps from his mother. Now as he became a star pupil, he also developed an unflattering arrogance to go along with his intelligence. Not surprisingly, considering the circumstances of his life at home, he was also an extremely proper young man. He adhered to a strict and rigid code of manners and was appalled when it was broken by fellow students whom he considered rude or boorish. He studied hard for hours, fixed his concentration on whatever task presented itself to him and otherwise seemed distracted or uninterested in the achievements and failures of others.

In high school, he was selective about the friends he made. A few of these friendships, however, proved to be deep and long lasting. One of these was with a boy in Oppenheimer's grade who had come to the school from Albuquerque, New Mexico. Francis Fergusson had been sent back East by his parents to attend high school in preparation for entering an Ivy League university. The two young men shared a common interest in philosophy and literature.

Oppenheimer also became a devoted friend and admirer of Herbert Smith, his English teacher at the school. Smith was a dynamic teacher who came to the school from Harvard University, where he was working toward a Ph.D. in English. By all accounts Smith made the study of English literature an entertaining endeavor, and he often invited his students back to his home, where they held long and heated discussions about ambitions and plans for the future.

During his final year in high school, Oppenheimer applied and was admitted to Harvard University. The summer after he graduated from high school, his family rewarded him with a trip to Germany. He spent a good deal of time there roaming the Hartz Mountains in search of mineral specimens. Oppenheimer, who was a tall, thin young man disdainful of sports and most physical exercise, did enjoy long solitary walks (as well as afternoons of sailing). The invigorating mountain air stimulated him, but unfortunately he also contracted a severe case of dysentery that summer, perhaps from impure drinking water from the mountain streams. The dysentery soon turned into colitis, a painful intestinal disorder. He was so sick on his return to the United States in the fall that he was unable to enroll at Harvard.

For months Oppenheimer was confined to bed at his parents' apartment in New York. Moody under even the best of circumstances, he became deeply depressed as a result of this period of confinement, going so far as to occasionally lock himself in his own room. It is possible that Oppenheimer felt a tremendous amount of stress about going off to Harvard. Colitis can result from stress, and it is conceivable that the nervous and success-driven Oppenheimer simply couldn't take the weight of being thrust out into the world away from the protective warmth of his family.

By spring, he had recovered enough to accept a suggestion from his father that he take a long trip in the summer through the West with Herbert Smith, his former English teacher. Julius Oppenheimer hoped that a sojourn into the spectacular mountains of Colorado and New Mexico would take Robert's mind off his troubles back East and set the stage for his return to college.

The trip, in the summer of 1922, was a great success. The wide open vistas of the West, especially the desert and mountain country of New Mexico, enchanted Oppenheimer. He took long rides on horseback with Herbert Smith, spending days at a time camping in the wilderness. He also looked up his school friend Francis Fergusson and became acquainted with one of Fergusson's friends, Paul Horgan, with whom he stumbled onto the town of Cowles in the Pecos River Valley of New Mexico. There Oppenheimer stayed at a guest ranch run by Winthrop and Katherine Page. Oppenheimer fell in love, apparently for the first time, with the fiery and beautiful Katherine Page. Oppenheimer charmed Page, who was considerably older than him, but she did not return the same degree of affection to him that he gave to her. Nonetheless, they began corresponding with each other and would be friends for many years.

In September, Oppenheimer returned east, stopping in New York before going up to Cambridge, Massachusetts, to enroll in Harvard. Oppenheimer plunged into the stimulating intellectual world offered by the university. He continued his studies in literature, concentrating especially on French writers. He also continued his studies of Greek and during his time at Harvard mastered that language.

By his second year, he decided to major in chemistry. At this time, he had no clear idea of his ultimate vocation in life, only a general inkling that it would somehow be in the sciences. "I remember," he told an interviewer later in his life, "talking to some older colleagues [at Harvard] as to whether I should study chemistry or . . . mineralogy with the idea of becoming a mining engineer because I loved that kind of life. . . . One of my friends said, 'Study chemistry; there are always summer vacations.'"

With those humorous marching orders, Oppenheimer began to bear down on his studies. He had little time for the usual extracurricular frolics. For a short while, he participated in a group that called itself the Liberal Club. This bunch was put off in an unfocused way by the mores and manners of life in the United States after World War I. In a magazine they published, called *The Gadfly*, they attacked what they saw as the smug, lazy attitudes of the 1920s, as exemplified by Presidents Harding and Coolidge. Oppenheimer also belonged to what he called a "science club," a small group of like-minded students and a few teachers who got together every now and again to discuss the latest advances in science and "philosophical questions relating to science."

Oppenheimer sailed through Harvard in three years rather than the customary four. During his last year and a half there, he discovered physics. The teacher most responsible for this awakening was a man named Percy Bridgman, an experimental physicist who would later become a Nobel Prize winner. Bridgman possessed a subtle and philosophically questioning mind that appealed to Oppenheimer. Bridgman was, in Oppenheimer's words, a "wonderful teacher because he never really was quite reconciled to things being the way they were and he always thought them out; his exercises were a good way to learn where the bones were in . . . physics . . . He was a man to whom one wanted to apprentice."

By his last year at Harvard, Oppenheimer had decided to study physics after his graduation. He knew this transition would prove difficult. He had from Bridgman only a beginner's knowledge of the subject, and his degree in chemistry was unlikely to impress world-class physicists at the leading European universities to which Oppenheimer had decided to apply for graduate study. On top of this, Oppenheimer had discovered from a semester-long project with Bridgman that he was not well suited for laboratory work. He enjoyed concepts and ideas, not working with machines and lab equipment. In spite of these drawbacks, he was determined to get on with learning physics, especially the newest branch, called quantum mechanics, that had turned all the theories of the past several hundred years upside down.

In the spring of 1925, Oppenheimer graduated from Harvard and asked Percy Bridgman for a letter of recommendation to help him gain admittance to Cambridge University in England. Cambridge was the leading center for the study of experimental physics. Never content to operate at the fringe, Oppenheimer had decided to plunge directly into the middle of the game.

CHAPTER 2 NOTES

p. 18   "She [Ella Oppenheimer] was a very delicate . . ." Alice Kimball Smith and Charles Weiner, eds., *Robert Oppenheimer: Letters and Recollections*, p. 2.

p. 22   "I remember . . ." interview with Thomas Kuhn, November 3, 1963, pp. 3-6.

p. 22   "wonderful teacher because . . ." Oppenheimer interview with Thomas Kuhn, November 3, 1963, pp. 9.

3
THE DISCIPLE

In September 1925, still unsure if he would be accepted into Cambridge University, Robert Oppenheimer left New York for England. The sea voyage to England took a week, which gave Oppenheimer time to compose a formal letter outlining his previous academic studies and requesting permission to enter Cambridge University as a graduate student. "I hope," he wrote, "at the end of three years, to take a degree of Doctor of Philosophy at the University. In preparation for this I should like to continue reading in Physics . . . ; and I should like, as soon as it seems advisable, to undertake a research problem in Physics."

Research, at least experimental research, was not Oppenheimer's strong suit, as Oppenheimer himself well knew. He was more inclined to ponder theoretical problems on paper than test them in the laboratory. But if he was to flourish at Cambridge, Oppenheimer would have to dirty his hands in the laboratory.

The crown jewel of Cambridge's scientific efforts was its famous Cavendish Laboratory, then, as now, one of the world's leading centers of research in nuclear physics. In 1925, Ernest Rutherford, perhaps the finest research physicist of the 20th century, directed the laboratory. Rutherford, who had won a Nobel Prize in 1908 for his study of radioactivity, was a physically robust and extroverted New Zealander who in many ways was Oppenheimer's opposite in background and temperament. Unlike Oppenheimer, Rutherford had grown up on the frontier. Born on an isolated farm, Rutherford as a youth rode horses and herded cattle to help his family. The schools he attended were newly founded and did not offer the latest in curriculum or laboratory equipment. In spite of these handicaps, Rutherford excelled in his studies, especially mathematics and physical sciences. He won scholarships that helped him attend the University of New Zealand and later Cambridge University. He arrived at Cambridge full of ambition and vigor in 1895. Rutherford's special talent lay in experimentation. He possessed a knack for discovering new ideas about the atom—and proving or disproving old ones—by experiments in his laboratory.

By the early part of the 20th century, physics had become a field increasingly divided between those who achieved most of their discoveries in the laboratory and those who made breakthroughs in ideas working alone or in small groups in an office. The former, the experimental physicists, enjoyed the comradeship of team effort required in the laboratory and the sheer physical joy of seeing with their own eyes the results of carefully crafted experiments. The latter, the theoretical physicists, preferred the contemplation of problems outside the lab, work they conducted largely with the aid of mathematics and by comparing different models through which they tried to explain such things as magnetism, light and the nature of the atom. By examining these models, or theories, both in the lab and mathematically, physicists hoped to explain how the physical world works—what matter is, what it is made of and how it functions in the universe.

Oppenheimer was fortunate to come to Europe to study physics in 1925. During the 30 years between 1895 and 1925 a revolution in physics, spearheaded by the leading European universities, had transformed humankind's understanding of the nature of matter. During this 30-year period, the existence of the atom as the essential building block of matter was definitively established, and a picture of its structure began to emerge.

The idea that everything in the universe is constructed out of single, infinitesimally small units, called atoms, goes back a long way in the Western world. This theory was first proposed in the fifth century B.C. by the Greek philosopher Democritus, and even though no one could produce a shred of evidence to support it, Democritus's theory, because it seemed to contain such common sense, was for centuries accepted by most scientists in Europe and later in America.

According to this view, the atom was the elemental building block from which everything in the universe was constructed. It was a single, complete object; there was nothing smaller than it; it had no bits and pieces from which it was made. It was like the brick used to construct a building. The building itself could be large or small, simple or complex, but the building was constructed of one basic element: the brick. So it was with the atom, from which everything else human and animal, stone and tree, even fire and water, is made. Different combinations of atoms produce different kinds of matter, but the single atom itself was seen always as being the same.

Scientists had faith in the idea of the atom. Nonetheless, the fact remained that even though they liked to believe that atoms were the basic elements of matter, no one had ever seen one, nor could anyone explain how atoms worked. For thousands of years, the atom was an idea like God: scientists wanted to believe in it, but no one could prove that it existed. Physicists considered the mystery of the atom to be the most important problem that confronted them during the late 19th and early 20th centuries.

Following Democritus, the theory of the atom was changed and refined by different generations of scientists. Isaac Newton, the great 17th-century English physicist, proposed an atom that was like a tiny billiard ball suspended in motion with other balls. "It seems probable to me," he wrote, "that God formed matter in solid, massy, hard, impenetrable, movable particles." Newton saw the universe as being like a machine, and his theories assumed that atoms were held together by mechanical laws.

To Newton, matter was composed of a collection of atoms held together by the force of gravity. Newton relied on gravity to explain how atoms worked because gravity was one of the forces of nature that had been uncovered and was well understood during his lifetime. Later, when electricity was better understood, atomic theory was changed to take this new phenomenon into account. James Clerk Maxwell, a physicist who discovered much about electromagnetism, proposed in 1873 a hard, solid atom held together by electromagnetic energy rather than mechanical energy such as gravity. Maxwell imagined the atom to be suspended in a void more or less the same way a pin might be held suspended in air between two magnets. In spite of this change in trying to understand the force that holds matter together, both Maxwell and Newton's theories imagine the atom as a solid, unbreakable object.

By the late 19th century, however, many scientists had begun to doubt that atoms existed at all. The concept worked well in chemistry, where it was used to explain how elements like oxygen and hydrogen could combine to make other substances (such as water, H_2O) but could not themselves be broken down any further. But by the mid-1800s, the mathematics of the mechanical model of atoms had come into conflict with the rules of another branch of physics, called thermodynamics. The conflict rested on the problem of reversibility. The mechanical model used by Newton, Maxwell and others assumed that events in the world were reversible. The mathematics and logic that backed up the mechanical model would not work if the world was not reversible. This, however, was contrary to the rules of thermodynamics—and common sense—which hold that some events, such as time, cannot be reversed. A German chemist explained the dilemma this way: "In a purely mechanical world, a tree could become a shoot and a seed again, the butterfly turn back into a caterpillar, and the old man into a child."

Understandably, the difference between the mechanical theory and what is observed in actual experience in the world caused a great deal of confusion in physics. As late as 1894, a mere 10 years before Robert Oppenheimer's birth, this contradiction had not been resolved. That year, Robert Cecil, chancellor of England's Oxford University, listed the unsolved questions pertaining to the atom. Humankind, he said, still had not discovered

What the atom of each element is, whether it is a movement, or a thing, or a vortex, or a point having inertia, whether there is any limit to its divisibility, and, if so, how that limit is imposed, whether the long list of elements is final. . . .

A clearer picture of what actually occurred at the atomic level only began to unfold as a result of a series of experiments conducted on seemingly unconnected problems in physics. From the information uncovered in these experiments, a clearer picture of the structure of the atom emerged.

In 1895, one year after Robert Cecil's catalogue of questions about the atom, the German physicist Wilhelm Röntgen (pronounced RENT-gen) stumbled on a discovery that refocused the attention of scientists around the world. Röntgen had been studying the unusual effects that occurred when electricity passed through a vacuum tube (an enclosed tube that has most of the air removed from it). Vacuum tubes had been studied by scientists for more than 40 years. A current of electricity entered the tube via two metal diodes (strips of metal at each end of the tube), causing a green fluorescent glow near the negatively charged diode. Scientists concocted various theories to explain this glow. The version accepted by most scientists speculated that the greenish glow was the visible indication of a force (perhaps made up of particles, although this could not yet be proved) that somehow was cast electrically from the atom (scientists were not sure which atoms this force came from but they theorized it originated from the atoms of the metal diode inside the tube, which was later proved to be true). Exactly how this force or these particles detached from the atom or how they related to the supposedly indivisible atom was as yet unclear.

Röntgen's experiment in 1895 was routine. He wanted to study the effect of the fluorescence inside a vacuum tube on certain chemicals. He expected no unusual findings. In his experiment, he had enclosed the vacuum tube inside a cardboard box. He had turned out the lights in his laboratory room to observe more clearly the fluorescence inside the enclosed box. He set up the experiment and turned on the electricity that flowed to the tube, which activated the glow in the vacuum.

He had watched the glow through a small hole for several minutes when he noticed something strange across the room. A number of feet away from the vacuum tube, but directly opposite it, Röntgen spied a glow on a screen that had been set up for another experiment. He walked over to look at the glow. It was just like the glow emitted on the inside of the vacuum tube. He switched the electricity off and the glow disappeared. He switched the electricity on again and put the screen in an adjoining room. The screen still glowed. This astonished Röntgen; whatever produced this glow obviously originated from the vacuum tube, and it penetrated not only the cardboard box around the tube but the wall of the room, too. Finally, with lights still off and the room darkened, Röntgen put his hand between the vacuum tube and the screen, and to his amazement, he saw projected on the screen the outline of the bones in his hand. His hand had become transparent; he could see through his skin and flesh to the skeleton inside.

Röntgen continued to study this mysterious phenomenon in secret for the next several weeks. Finally he published a paper

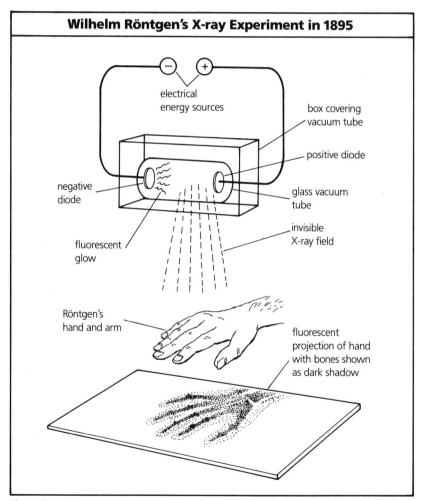

Wilhelm Röntgen's X-ray Experiment in 1895

electrical energy sources

box covering vacuum tube

positive diode

negative diode

glass vacuum tube

fluorescent glow

invisible X-ray field

Röntgen's hand and arm

fluorescent projection of hand with bones shown as dark shadow

Figure 1

about it in a scientific journal, naming the effect for the first time. He believed he had discovered a new kind of particle that was emitted from the atom. He called this particle the X ray.

Röntgen's discovery caused a sensation not only among scientists but with the public as well. Kings and queens of the various European countries called in their physicists and demanded a demonstration of the X ray. Physicians, too, immediately realized that the X ray could be used to help them diagnose the conditions of their patients.

New discoveries about the atom began to follow rapidly one after the other now. In 1897, an English physicist named J. J. Thompson, who also had conducted studies of the fluorescence inside vacuum tubes, managed with the aid of a magnet to bend the path of the force passing through a vacuum tube. In another experiment, he bent the path of the force with a current of electricity. By doing this, he proved the force that created the fluorescence was a particle, and because of the way it reacted to the magnet, he demonstrated that the particle possessed a negative charge. He named this particle the "negative corpuscle"; today it is known as the electron, the extremely light, fast particle that whirls around the mass of the atom.

Still other studies followed Röntgen's discovery of the X ray as scientists scrambled to understand the meaning of fluorescence. If the fluorescence inside a vacuum tube could produce X rays, could other naturally fluorescent materials produce X rays, too? Several substances were tried, but none worked. However, scientists soon discovered one that did: uranium, in the form of the mineral uranium potassium sulfate. Soon this phenomenon, whereby a substance emitted particle radiation, was named; it was dubbed *radioactivity.* The hunt now shifted to identifying and chemically extracting the elements that produced these effects. The most determined researchers in this endeavor were the French scientists Marie and Pierre Curie.

Marie Curie devised an instrument, called an electrometer, that detected radiation emitted from substances. Then she began systematically to check numerous ores and minerals to determine which ones were radioactive. In this way she uncovered all kinds of previously unknown compounds. Slowly she began to separate these compounds chemically to try to determine if they were elements. Elements are fundamental substances, such as gold, oxygen or carbon, that consist of atoms of only one kind and that form the basic materials of the universe. Scientists already knew that uranium and thorium were elements, but chemists had long predicted that elements, which some day would be discovered, were missing in the periodic table (the chart that lists all the basic atomic materials).

The process of extracting one compound from another until the essence of the compound, the element, has been gathered in its purest form was painstaking and took many years of Marie Curie's life. However, her first breakthroughs came quickly. In 1898, Marie and Pierre Curie announced the discovery of two new elements, both of which were radioactive, which they named polonium (after Marie Curie's native Poland) and radium.

During subsequent experiments with these radioactive materials, Marie Curie also discovered another important property of these kinds of elements. She noticed that over a period of time the radioactivity of radium, thorium and other similar elements decreased.

At this point, Robert Oppenheimer's future teacher, Ernest Rutherford, entered the search for the meaning of the atom. Rutherford had been at Cambridge in England for only three years when, in 1898, he began experiments on Marie Curie's newly found property of radioactivity. After a year and a half of study of thorium and radium, he discovered that these and other radioactive elements transmuted, or decayed, into other elements. Rutherford set this process of radioactive decay in a time frame, which he dubbed the *half-life*. The half-life describes the period of time in which half of the original sample of the element changes into another element. For instance, some forms of polonium possess a half-life of 27 days. Uranium, on the other hand, has a half-life of 4.5 billion years. Both polonium and uranium decay to lead, the closest stable element near them in the periodic table, so that, for example, after 4.5 billion years a gram of pure uranium would consist of .5 gram uranium and .5 gram of lead. After another 4.5 billion years it would consist of .25 gram uranium and .75 lead. The decay continues in this manner, the element losing one-half of its weight during each half-life, until eventually only an infinitesimal amount of the radioactive element is left.

In his studies of radioactive decay, Rutherford became interested in identifying the particles that are radiated by elements like uranium, that is, Wilhelm Röntgen's still mysterious X rays. Quickly Rutherford discovered that X rays are in fact made up of several different kinds of radiation. Two of these types Rutherford named after the first two letters of the Greek alphabet: alpha and beta rays.

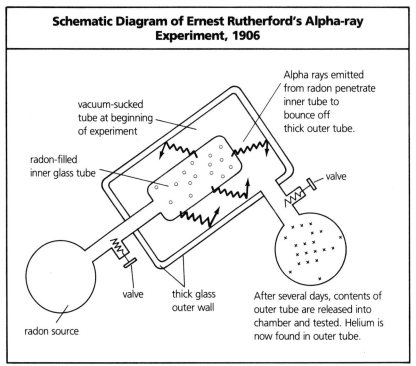

Schematic Diagram of Ernest Rutherford's Alpha-ray Experiment, 1906

Alpha rays emitted from radon penetrate inner tube to bounce off thick outer tube.

vacuum-sucked tube at beginning of experiment

radon-filled inner glass tube

valve

valve   thick glass outer wall

radon source

After several days, contents of outer tube are released into chamber and tested. Helium is now found in outer tube.

Figure 2

Rutherford devised an elegant experiment to determine the nature of the alpha ray. He constructed two glass bulbs, one inside the other. The inner bulb he filled with radon gas, which was known to emit abundant amounts of alpha particles. The outer bulb was sucked clean of all gases, that is, a vacuum was established inside it. The wall of the inner bulb was thin enough to allow alpha particles to penetrate it, yet the wall of the outer bulb was thick enough to stop the alpha rays. In this way, Rutherford hoped to trap the essence of the alpha rays inside the outer bulb. After several days, Rutherford examined the contents of the outer bulb and found that it now contained helium. Helium, the second lightest element, is composed of two protons and two neutrons. In this way, Rutherford proved that alpha particles were bundles of two protons and two neutrons that were ejected from unstable, radioactive elements. Alpha rays are much heavier and slower than other types of radiation, and therefore are more easily stopped by solid objects or liquids. Rutherford also confirmed that beta rays are electrons thrown from the atom. Beta rays are lighter and faster than alpha rays and can penetrate heavier materials. The final element of X rays was discovered in the 1930s. They are called gamma rays. Gamma rays, virtually weightless bursts of energy, are lighter and faster than either alpha or beta rays.

One of Rutherford's greatest experiments, conducted in 1910, proved the existence of the nucleus of the atom, and thus the existence of the atom itself. He directed a stream of alpha particles at a 45° angle toward a thin sheet of gold foil. He and his assistants expected that the alpha particles would shoot straight through the foil, yet to their great surprise a number of the alpha rays appeared to bounce off the foil. Their impact was recorded on a screen positioned on the side of the foil opposite the alpha source.

Because Rutherford knew the speed and weight of the alpha particle he could calculate the magnetic energy required to bend it from a straight path. The total was an enormous figure. "It was quite the most incredible event that has ever happened to me," he wrote. "It was almost as incredible as if you fired a 15-inch [artillery] shell at a piece of tissue paper and it came back and hit you. On consideration I realized that this scattering backwards [bouncing off the gold foil] must be the result of a single collision, and when I made the calculations I saw that it was impossible to get anything of that order unless you took a system in which the greatest part of the mass of the atom was concentrated in a minute nucleus."

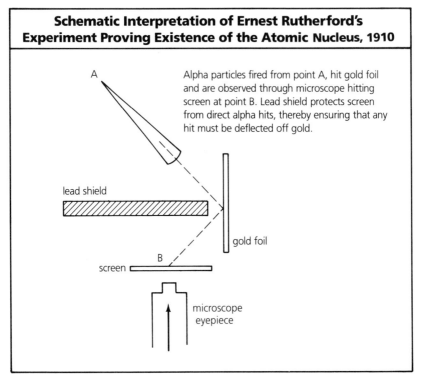

Figure 3

In this indirect fashion, by drawing deductions from the results of experimental research, physicists had begun to form a picture of the atom.

The discovery of X rays, electrons, radioactivity and the atomic nucleus helped unveil many of the secrets of the atom, yet a larger overview of the structure of the atom and the rules of its behavior still eluded scientists. For instance, no one could yet satisfactorily explain how the atom was actually held together. It was known that electrons were negatively charged particles with a very small weight or mass. Further, Rutherford had demonstrated that atomic nuclei were much heavier objects, positively charged and possessing tremendous electromagnetic energy. Thus the question remained: How could these two units and specifically two electrons orbiting a nucleus, hold themselves together to form an atom? Why did they not instead simply fly apart or collapse into one another as two magnets of positive and negative charges will grip one another when put together at close range?

Newton's old mechanical laws, based on gravity, could not explain how the atom held itself together. Yet, clearly, the atom was stable. Experimental evidence showed how rock-stable it was. How could this be explained?

This dilemma was only resolved when scientists began to understand the atom as being not a hard, fixed object like a billiard ball, but a unit of electrical and magnetic energy whose actions could be understood in terms of probabilities. The job of unraveling experimental data and interpreting it in a way that made sense fell primarily to theoretical physicists, most notably the Danish physicist Niels Bohr.

To explain the forces holding the atom together, Bohr had to drop totally the old ideas of the atom. He could not use preconceived notions about the atom; instead he used only experimental data. He did not attempt to explain why the data indicated certain things happening inside the atom (he couldn't do this). Instead, he simply accepted the data as his guide. The data would help him unravel the mechanics of the atom.

He began work first on one of the most striking peculiarities of the atom: the way the electrons orbiting the nucleus moved from one energy state to another when they were heated. The old laws of physics indicated that when matter was heated, which added energy to its atoms, its electrons should show regular, steady increases in its orbit around the nucleus. Yet experimental evidence clearly demonstrated that this did not happen. Instead electrons jumped from one level to another, often skipping levels predicted by Newtonian laws. This uneven jump in orbit perplexed physicists.

Bohr, however, offered an explanation for this orbital jump, based on the work of a German physicist named Max Planck. Bohr explained these jumps as being examples of quanta, packets of energy absorbed by atoms when they are heated. To firm up his hypothesis, Bohr looked to chemistry, from which he borrowed the spectrograms of various elements. A spectrum is the record of

the light emitted by every compound as seen after it is passed
through a prism. The prism breaks the light given off by the
compound into a unique series of lines. Becasue each compound
in nature has a distinctive pattern of lines, the composition of
any material can be deduced from its spectrum. Also, the spectrum clearly indicates jumps or spaces between the various lines
of the spectrum. Until Bohr, no one had clearly understood why
these jumps existed. Bohr compared spectrograms of hydrogen
to Planck's calculations about quanta and showed that the two
matched perfectly. Energy absorbed by an atom was indicated
by the jumps shown in the spectrum. To absorb energy, the
electrons jumped from one position to the next. Some of these
jumps were farther than others, and each one took the electron
farther away from the nucleus of the atom. When the atom
cooled or lost energy, the electrons jumped back to the beginning position, which Bohr labeled the "steady state" because it
clearly indicated the orbit the electron fell into in order to
preserve the stability of the atom.

Bohr could not explain why the electrons chose to jump from
one position to another. He simply accepted that this was so and
offered the explanation that the level "chosen" by the electrons
was a result of the law of probabilities. This explanation marked
a radically new approach to physics. Before Bohr, physicists had
tried to make the atom fit models that worked for larger objects,
such as the way gravity worked in explaining the orbits of planets
around the sun. After Bohr, the atom was explained on its own
terms from the experimental evidence gathered about it by physicists and chemists.

Bohr's theories, along with those of Albert Einstein and others,
backed by the experiments of Rutherford and his tribe of experimental physicists, represented the cutting edge of humankind's
understanding of the atom at the time Robert Oppenheimer came
to England in 1925. The atom was now seen, not as a solid object,
but essentially as tremendously compressed fields of energy, little
tornadoes composed of enormous amounts of electromagnetic
energy. Likewise, matter itself was thought of as essentially empty
space, inhabited here and there by fields of energy, called atoms.
The atoms themselves were not whole, unbreakable objects but

were composed of parts and pieces of energy, all of which related to the whole, but occasionally separated from it, too. By forcing separations of the parts from the whole, physicists were able to learn still more about the structure and workings of the atom.

Oppenheimer arrived in England full of naive optimism about his future. At this point in his life, he was an apprentice chemist who had decided to turn to physics. Percy Bridgman's letter to Ernest Rutherford did little to persuade Rutherford to admit Oppenheimer as a student at the Cavendish Laboratory. Nonetheless, Oppenheimer was relentless in his pleading for admittance, and by the beginning of the fall term Rutherford agreed to let him into the lab.

Oppenheimer was assigned to work with the lab's former director and one of its older physicists, J. J. Thompson, the discoverer of the electron. Oppenheimer did not do well in the tedious physical chores that were necessary in the lab. "I am having a pretty bad time," he wrote his Harvard friend Francis Fergusson. "The lab work is a terrible bore, and I am so bad at it that it is impossible to feel that I am learning anything."

Robert Oppenheimer had never failed in an academic endeavor before, and his feeling of being involved in something that was simultaneously tedious and over his head began to fill him with anxiety and dread. Things got so bad that at one point he wrote Herbert Smith, his mentor at the School for Ethical Culture, that he was "on the point of bumping [himself] off."

At Christmas, Oppenheimer and Francis Fergusson met in Paris for a vacation (Fergusson was attending Oxford that same year). It was supposed to be a lighthearted holiday away from the tense academic environment in England. But Oppenheimer could not let go of his disappointment and mounting alarm over his schoolwork. Toward the end of the vacation, without provocation, he leaped onto Fergusson and tried to strangle him. Fergusson, much larger than the skinny Oppenheimer, easily knocked him away. Oppenheimer left Paris immediately, and later wrote Fergusson a letter of apology. But the incident indicated to Fergusson just how disturbed his friend had become.

Back at Cambridge, Oppenheimer determinedly pushed ahead, reading in physics late into the night after he had finished a full day's worth of lab work. Sometime during the winter of 1926, he met Niels Bohr for the first time. The great Danish physicist had come to Cambridge to visit his old teacher, Ernest Rutherford, and as usual, Bohr poked around the laboratory to see what each of the students was up to. Bohr's kindly presence seemed to reassure Oppenheimer; it also added to his growing realization that he was better suited for theoretical rather than experimental physics.

At about this time, Oppenheimer began to visit a psychiatrist to seek treatment for his emotional problems. The psychiatrist diagnosed Oppenheimer as suffering from dementia praecox, a concept used then for what is now known as schizophrenia. Oppenheimer's prognosis, according to the psychiatrist, was not favorable. At the time, dementia praecox was considered an incurable disease that eventually would require permanent hospitalization.

Alarmed at the news of their son's health, Oppenheimer's mother and father traveled to England. At Easter break, they persuaded Robert to vacation with two of his Cambridge friends in Corsica, a French island in the Mediterranean Sea. This journey, much like the one he had taken to New Mexico in 1922, seemed to calm him. One reason for this was that Oppenheimer apparently had a love affair, the first one of his life, with a young woman he met in Corsica. So important and essential was this liaison, that Oppenheimer, who could be a secretive man, refused to discuss it later in his life. He would say only that it was "not a mere love affair, not a love affair at all, but love."

Oppenheimer returned to Cambridge and finished his year there. Then he transferred to the University of Göttingen in Germany, one of the premier centers in Europe for theoretical physics. To the degree that he had suffered in Cambridge, Oppenheimer flourished in Göttingen. For one thing, his year at the Cavendish Laboratory had allowed him time to begin to grasp the new ideas in physics, ones to which he had only barely been introduced in America. Neils Bohr's ideas about quanta and steady states were at the forefront of physics in 1926. This school of thought, known as quantum mechanics, dominated the University of Göttingen, and Oppenheimer eagerly plunged in to learn as much about it as he could.

Oppenheimer's teacher in Göttingen was the distinguished physicist Max Born, later a Nobel laureate. Göttingen in those days was filled with future Nobel Prize winners. Wolfgang Pauli, Werner Heisenberg and Enrico Fermi were the trio of future laureates whom Oppenheimer either met or studied with during his stay in Göttingen.

Between 1926 and 1929, his last year in Europe, Oppenheimer publihsed 16 papers on the physics of quantum mechanics. His papers, which were densely mathematical and difficult for a nonphysicist to understand, used the concepts of quantum theory to focus on different aspects of the atom, such as electron spin, or the idea that the electron itself spins on its own axis as it moves around the nucleus in the same way the Earth spins as it moves around the sun. The concept of electron spin helped physicists resolve questions about how the atom binds itself together.

Oppenheimer was granted a doctorate in physics, "with distinction," in 1927 from the University of Göttingen. He returned to the United States for the academic year 1927–28 and received a grant from the National Research Council of the United States to teach and continue his studies in America and abroad. To this end, he spent the 1927–28 academic year teaching first at Harvard, then in California, where he taught at the University of California at Berkeley and the California Institute of Technology in Los Angeles.

In the spring of 1928, his health began to bother him again. He had become a heavy smoker by then and had developed a troublesome cough that would not go away. He was diagnosed as suffering from tuberculosis and told to set aside time immediately for rest and recovery. With his brother Frank, he returned again to the mountains of New Mexico. Together they happened upon a small parcel of land on which an old log cabin had been built. The land was up for lease. Charmed with the cabin and its idylic setting, the Oppenheimer brothers immediately bought the lease. After a few days' thought, they named the place Perro Caliente, Spanish for "Hot Dog."

The two brothers spent a happy and relaxed summer there before Robert returned to Europe in September. During the next year he used the last of his grant money to polish his mathematical skills, first in the Netherlands with the physicist Paul Ehrenfest and later in Switzerland with Wolfgang Pauli, a mentor from his days at Göttingen. At the end of this stint, he returned to the United States, this time for good.

He had come a long way from the unconfident and troubled young man he had been on his arrival in Cambridge in 1925. In his understanding of physics, he was now the equal of anyone in the world, and he was eager to teach what he knew to his fellow countrymen. In Europe, he had spoken to colleagues of a dream of establishing a center that would be second to none in the study of physics. Now, on his return to the United States, he had a chance to fulfill this dream. A number of distinguished colleges and universities offered him jobs, but the place he chose seemed to many of his friends an unlikely spot. He decided to head west to the University of California at Berkeley, a relatively undistinguished state university, one that was neither as old nor as prestigious as the Ivy League schools. There Robert Oppenheimer would seek to build a name and a new life for himself.

CHAPTER 3 NOTES

p. 24   "I hope at the end of three years . . ." Alice Kimball Smith and Charles Weiner, eds., *Robert Oppenheimer: Letters and Recollections,* p. 84.

p. 27   "What the atom of each element is . . ." quoted in James Chadwick, The Rutherford Memorial Lecture, *Proceedings of the Royal Society of Science*, vol. 224, p. 435.

p. 33   "It was quite the most . . . " quoted in G. K. T. Conn and H. D. Turner, *The Evolutin of the Nuclear Atom*, p. 136.

p. 37   "I am having . . ." Alice Kimball Smith and Charles Weiner, eds., *Robert Oppenheimer: Letters and Recollections,* p. 87.

4

AN OASIS IN THE DESERT

In the fall of 1929, Robert Oppenheimer, only 25 years old, moved to Berkeley to become professor of physics at the University of California. He also accepted a position as a part-time professor at the California Institute of Technology, located in the Los Angeles suburb of Pasadena. The move to California was a natural decision for Oppenheimer. California appealed to all of his instincts. Its pleasant climate attracted him, and California's "westerness" delighted him. The West promised a radically different life from the rather dull and protected one he had had back East in New York and at Harvard. In the West he could at last grow up, separate himself from his parents and become his own man. For these reasons, California signaled a fresh, clean start to his life back in the United States.

The Berkeley faculty of physics also offered Oppenheimer a chance to spread the gospel of the new physics, which had not yet penetrated into the faculties and courses of most American universities. When Oppenheimer returned to Europe for a year-long visit in 1927 and 1928, he spoke openly of wanting to create a department of physics that would rival any in Europe. He conceived of this mission as taming "the desert" because to him American universities were like deserts in their isolated and outdated approach to science, especially to physics. Now, at the University of California, he imagined he had his very own desert to play with, and he began immediately to irrigate it with his vigor and imagination.

On his arrival at Berkeley, Oppenheimer was surprised to learn the he wasn't the only member of the physics faculty to harbor large ambitions. Another new arrival, Ernest Lawrence, had already busied himself constructing huge and complicated machines, called cyclotrons, used to smash the nucleus of the atom. By breaking apart the atomic nucleus, physicists could observe and classify the types of particles that constituted this core of atomic structure. For this reason cyclotrons offered themselves as a new and exciting experimental tool with which theories about atomic composition could be tested.

In most ways, Lawrence and Oppenheimer were opposites. Lawrence was a midwestern Protestant from a small town in South Dakota, whereas Oppenheimer was a Jewish New Yorker. Lawrence loved tinkering on machines; Oppenheimer was always a man who valued theory over work in the lab. Lawrence was a political conservative; Oppenheimer soon became politically active and adopted many left-wing political attitudes. Yet in spite of these differences, the two men got on well and seemed to complement each other's skills and personalities.

Lawrence and Oppenheimer's friendship was remarkable because Oppenheimer was not known for getting along well with colleagues. By the time he arrived in California, Oppenheimer had become even more harsh and judgmental of others than he had been in his youth. He was quick at seeing and being able to go to the core of any problem, but he could be haughty and scornful of those who were not as swift as he or who preferred a different approach. Yet, at the same time, he encouraged and inspired a small band of graduate students in physics, a group that became known as "Oppie's boys." "Robert found it very difficult to form proper relationships with equals," one colleague remarked. "He could be respectful and deferential to one or two people like [Albert] Einstein, and he was happy to have adoring pupils at his feet. Anything else, there were problems."

Oppenheimer's abrasiveness was clearly demonstrated in an encounter he had with James Franck, one of his former teachers at Göttingen. Franck had traveled to Berkeley to give a lecture with the grandiose title "Fundamental Meaning of Quantum Mechanics." Later, during a talk given by one of Oppenheimer's graduate students, Franck asked a question that Oppenheimer considered insufficiently penetrating. Oppenheimer directed an unnecessarily stinging comment toward Franck by interjecting: "I don't mean to deliver any lectures on the Fundamental Meaning of Quantum Mechanics, but the meaning of that question is a foolish one." Tragically, Oppenheimer recognized the self-destructiveness of this flaw in his character, which he termed "the beastliness," but often he could not prevent himself from indulging in it.

In spite of his prickliness, Oppenheimer quickly attracted many of the brightest students in the physics department. Like Herbert Smith, his English teacher at the School for Ethical Culture, Oppenheimer did not separate his personal life from those of his students. He often treated his students to wine and dinner at Jack's Restaurant, a popular eatery in San Francisco, and on the weekends many of these same young men could be found discussing physics, literature, art and music at his apartment back in Berkeley. "He was the first person who made physics more than a set of rules," one student remembered of Oppenheimer. "He made it a matter of quarrying knowledge from nature." Hans Bethe, who got to know Oppenheimer as a fellow faculty member at Berkeley in the late 1930s, said, "Probably the most important ingredient [Oppenheimer] brought to his teaching was his exquisite taste. He always knew what were the important problems, as shown by his choice of subjects. He truly lived with those problems, struggling for a solution, and he communicated his concern to his group."

One month after Oppenheimer moved to California, the New York stock market crashed and brought down with it the American economy. By 1933, many of the nation's banks had failed, innumerable businesses had gone bankrupt and more than a quarter of the country's workers were unemployed. During the early thirties, Oppenheimer was largely unaware of the suffering cause by this economic collapse, called the Great Depression. He didn't own a radio, didn't have a telephone and never read newspapers or popular magazines. He didn't even learn of the stock market crash until six months after it had occurred, when Ernest Lawrence happened to mention it to him in conversation. Furthermore, besides his income derived from teaching, Oppenheimer received a generous yearly allowance from a trust fund set up by his father. He lived well and his concerns—science, literature, art, philosophy—were high-minded. He later admitted that he "was interested in man and his experience, but had no understanding of the relations of man to his society."

By 1936, however, not even Oppenheimer could ignore the suffering inflicted on his compatriots by the depression. By that date, the economic hardships had begun to affect his students directly. Many had to take menial jobs on which their talent and training were wasted; others could find no work at all. "Through them," Oppenheimer said of his students, "I began to understand how deeply political and economic events could affect men's lives. I began to feel the need to participate more fully in the life of the community."

Also at this time Oppenheimer began to sense a rising danger abroad. By 1936, Adolf Hitler had been *Führer*, or absolute dictatorial ruler, of Germany for three years, and through his government's anti-Semitic policies he persecuted the Jews of Germany, among them Robert Oppenheimer's relatives. Also, Hitler's party, the Nazis, had led Germany into the civil war in Spain, siding with the conservative General Francisco Franco against the democratically elected socialist government. For thoughtful people in Europe and America, both of these events cast a shadow over the future.

Slowly, Oppenheimer began to seek out groups on the Berkeley campus that agitated for economic and political change. Oppenheimer, who was so self-assured and arrogant in almost ever aspect of his life, felt out of his league in politics. By the spring of 1936, however, he had found someone to guide him, someone with whom he also fell in love.

Her name was Jean Tatlock. She was a graduate student in psychology at the university, and her father was a professor of medieval literature on the Berkeley campus. Tatlock had been an on-and-off member of the Communist Party for several years before she met Oppenheimer, and she introduced him to her friends, many of whom were also members of the party. Through Jean Tatlock, Oppenheimer plunged into radical politics in California. He joined the radical Teachers' Union, which agitated for better pay for graduate teaching assistants and spent a great deal of debate on ineffectual resolutions dealing with world problems far beyond their control. Oppenheimer also joined a number of other organizations that were secretly controlled by members of the Communist Party, but it is unclear if he ever became a party member himself. All of this activity was out in the open on Oppenheimer's part. "I became a real left-winger," he was to say later. "[I] joined the Teachers' Union, had lots of Communist friends. It was what most people do in college or late high school . . . but I'm not ashamed of it. I'm more ashamed of its lateness. Most of what I believed then, now seems complete nonsense, but it was an essential part of becoming a whole man."

During this period of reassessment, Oppenheimer made another close friend with ties to radical politics. His name was Haakon Chevalier, and he was an instructor of French literature (always one of Oppenheimer's favorite subjects) at the University of California and president of the Teachers' Union there. Chevalier also guided Oppenheimer in political matters, even though Chevalier was awed by Oppenheimer's intellectual prowess in other fields. Chevalier remembered Oppenheimer as a complex man, full of contradictions:

> He was tall, nervous, and intent, and he moved with an odd gait, a kind of jog, with a great deal of swinging of his limbs, his head always a little to one side, one shoulder higher than the other. But it was the head that was most striking: the halo of wispy black curly hair, the fine, sharp nose, and especially the eyes, surprisingly blue, having a strange depth and intensity. . . . He looked like a young Einstein and at the same time an overgrown choirboy. There was something both subtly wise and terribly innocent about his face.

Throughout the 1930s, Oppenheimer continued theoretical work on quantum physics. He wrote a number of papers about positrons (positively charged electrons, which were discovered by Carl Anderson, a colleague of Oppenheimer at Cal Tech) and cosmic rays (high-energy radiation originating from sources deep in space). From his observation of cosmic rays and other atomic phenomena, Oppenheimer speculated about the existence of collapsed stars of small size and huge density. The existence of these so-called black holes could not be proved for another 40 years, until the instruments to detect them had been invented.

However, despite this work and his great initial promise, demonstrated in Göttingen and later in the Netherlands and Zurich,

Robert Oppenheimer at Berkeley. (J. Robert Oppenheimer Memorial Committee)

Oppenheimer did not succeed in making discoveries in the 1930s that were at the cutting edge of his field. His colleagues still considered him an excellent physicist, one who had a thorough and profound grasp of the latest atomic theory, but they did not think of him as being at the very top rank of theorists, those who actually pushed back the limits of humankind's knowledge of the atom. None of these men and women believed that Oppenheimer would ever win the Nobel Prize, the ultimate symbol of success in physics.

"He was a dilettante," one of his graduate students said of him. "He just would not take his coat off and really get stuck in. He'd got ability, certainly, but he hadn't got the staying power."

Another colleague, I. I. Rabi, who eventually did win a Nobel Prize for his work identifying particles within the atomic nucleus, said of Oppenheimer:

[He] was overeducated in those fields which lie outside the scientific tradition, such as his interest in religion, in the Hindu religion in particular, which resulted in a feeling of mystery of the universe that surrounded him almost like a fog. He saw physics clearly, looking toward what had already been done, but at the border he tended to feel there was much more of the mysterious and novel than there actually was. . . . [He turned] away from the hard, crude methods of theoretical physics into a mystical realm of broad intuition.

In spite of this assessment of his research skills, by the late 1930s Oppenheimer, along with Ernest Lawrence, had managed to create a center for the study of physics that was second to none in the world. Oppenheimer's students now were truly first-rate. They were a varied crew. Philip Morrison had overcome polio and the poverty of the small California town in which he had grown up to become an excellent apprentice physicist. Rossi Lomanitz came to Berkeley from Oklahoma at the age of 14, a "wide-eyed boy from the sticks." Bernard Peters, a German Jew, had escaped from the Dachau concentration camp, fled to America and worked as a longshoreman in New York before coming to study in California.

By 1936, Oppenheimer's brother Frank also had come west to Cal Tech in Pasadena to study physics. Frank idolized his brother and copied what he did, but he could never equal his brother in physics. Like Robert, Frank also became active in radical politics in California, and soon, apparently unlike Robert, he joined the Communist Party.

During the 1930s, working for the Communist Party was not considered to be an ill-advised move for many young students and intellectuals in the United States. Communists were numerous and visible in many big American cities. The issues they pressed for—racial integration; fair wages for working people; an end to unemployment; support of governments such as those of China, France and the Soviet Union that stood up to Germany and Japan—were popular with many Americans. Also, the evils of Joseph Stalin's government inside the Soviet Union—the political repression and massive system of forced labor camps—were not well understood by many Americans at this time.

Besides his own personal work for various left-wing groups in California, Oppenheimer read voraciously about politics. One book that especially impressed him was a work praising the achievements of the Soviet Union by Sydney and Beatrice Webb, entitled *Soviet Communism: A New Civilization*. The Webbs' book painted a bright picture of communism. However, by 1938 Oppenheimer was shown a different view when he was visited by two scientists he knew and respected, Victor Weisskopf and George Placzek, who had just returned from a visit to the Soviet Union. Weisskopf and Placzek described a very different Soviet Union from that seen by the Webbs. To the two scientists, Stalin's regime seemed very much like the Nazi fascist government under Hitler in Germany. They told Oppenheimer about the lack of personal freedoms, rigged trials and rough treatment of scientists (or anyone else) who disagreed with the government's views. After listening to his two friends, Oppenheimer's uncritical support of the Soviet Union and the American Communist Party began slowly to change.

Oppenheimer's love affair with Jean Tatlock continued for another year and a half. At one point they became engaged, then Tatlock, a tumultous person, began to disappear for long periods of time without warning. Later, she would torment Oppenheimer by telling him that she had been seeing other men. They argued and made up. Then they fought again. Tatlock began seeing a psychiatrist because she felt depressed and at a loss with what to do with her life. By 1939, she and Oppenheimer had broken off, although he had not completely gotten over his love for her and still communicated with her occasionally.

Later that year, during a teaching stint at Cal Tech, Oppenheimer met a woman who almost made him forget Jean Tatlock. Kitty Puening, who also was involved in leftist politics, was unhappily married at the time to a British physician, Dr. Richard Harrison. Puening's marriage to Harrison was her third. (She had been married for a very short period to a musician during the time she had been a student in France in 1933, and later she had been married to Joe Dallet, an American Communist who was killed in 1937 fighting for the Republican government in Spain.) Puening and Oppenheimer were immediately attracted to each other, and they began to see one another whenever Oppenheimer came to Los Angeles to teach. Richard Harrison soon became aware of what was going on. He also wanted out of the marriage to Kitty but hoped to delay a divorce until his medical career was more firmly established. The following summer, Kitty visited Oppenheimer at his Perro Caliente Ranch in New Mexico. Dr. Harrison remained in California. By November, Puening had obtained a divorce, and on November 1, 1940, she married Robert Oppenheimer.

Robert Oppenheimer's life in Berkeley began to change noticeably soon after his marriage to Kitty. He moved out of his bachelor apartment and bought a house, a place he named Eagle Hill, for himself and Kitty. His attendance at political events decreased; he went out with his students less; he became more of a homebody. Still he did not entirely cut politics out of his life. The Nazis had overrun France in June 1940, an event that upset Oppenheimer, a committed Francophile, terribly. Also, Oppenheimer became active that year in a new organization for scientists, the American Association of Scientific Workers, a group of scientists who got together to talk about the role of scientists in a democratic society.

Later that year, an old friend of Kitty arrived in the Bay area. His name was Steve Nelson, and he was a full-time organizer for the Communist Party. The Oppenheimers saw Nelson and their friends the Chevaliers often at parties and political meetings in San Francisco and Berkeley during the next year and a half. It was a wonderful time for Oppenheimer. He seemed to have mellowed somewhat. He was noted for his charm at the parties he hosted and became famous for the spicy martinis he loved to make for guests. Best of all, he and Kitty had a son, Peter, born in May 1941.

In June 1941, German armies invaded the Soviet Union, an event that persuaded Oppenheimer and many others that it would only be a matter of time before the United States was dragged into what was becoming a worldwide war. Unbeknownst to Oppenheimer, the U.S. government had begun to investigate what seemed like a far-fetched proposition: that a new weapon, a superbomb, could be constructed that would help to protect the United States in the event it entered the war. This weapon would utilize the phenomenon of fission, the splitting of the atom, which atomic scientists had demonstrated as an actual occurrence—not a theoretical speculation—in experiments in Germany in 1938. The idea of an atomic bomb had occurred to Oppenheimer as far back as 1938, soon after news of the discovery of fission. One of his students, Philip Morrison, recalls that "within perhaps a week [after the news about fission] there was on the blackboard in Robert Oppenheimer's office a drawing—a very bad, an execrable drawing—of a bomb."

By the autumn of 1941, Oppenheimer had begun to chafe with his life in Berkeley. He loved Kitty and delighted in his new family, but he felt that he had not really contributed much to the defeat of the Nazi regime, which he now saw as the main enemy of the democratic countries of the world. Many of Oppenheimer's students and colleagues had left their academic positions to engage in military research, most notably to develop the radar that helped the British defeat the German air force during the Battle of Britain in the summer of 1940. Oppenheimer wanted to join them, but he did not yet know how to do this. In October 1941, Ernest Lawrence invited Oppenheimer to come along with him to a secret meeting of scientists being held at the laboratories of the General Electric Company in Schenectady, New York. Before this meeting, Lawrence warned Oppenheimer that he should resign from the American Association of Scientific Workers (AASW), which Lawrence saw as a radical organization. "I know nothing wrong with it," he told Oppenheimer, "but we're planning big things in connection with the war effort, and it wouldn't be right [for Oppenheimer to remain a member of the AASW]. I want no occasion for somebody in Washington to find fault with us." The meeting, Oppenheimer learned, was one of the first get-togethers of top scientists who were trying to figure out how to build a superbomb, which they dubbed an atomic bomb, out of fissionable material such as uranium. The process of building the bomb would be mind-bogglingly complex, but a number of scientists had demanded that action on the project begin immediately.

Oppenheimer was curious about the meeting and pleased to have been invited. What he did not then realize was that he had almost been banned from the project because of what Lawrence termed his "leftwandering activities." Lawrence, however, persuaded the others that Oppenheimer was a loyal citizen and should be included on the team. In preparation for the meeting, Oppenheimer drew up quick calculations that showed the amount of uranium needed to build an explosive weapon. He figured the amount to be approximately 100 kilograms (about 220 pounds, a figure that later proved to be too high). The problem was complicated because not just any type of uranium could be used. The fission experiments in 1938 had clearly demonstrated that only one isotope (or variant) of uranium produced a high enough rate of fission, or atom-splitting, to be suitable bomb material. This isotope was called uranium 235 (its symbol in the periodic table is U-235). Uranium 235 could only be extracted from uranium ore after a long and difficult process of refinement. As of 1941, only minute amounts (fractions of a gram) had been extracted. Scientists saw they would need not pinheads of U-235 but wheelbarrows of it. The scientists discussed how much time they would need to produce that amount of U-235. No one had a ready answer. This type of manufacturing had never been done before. In a pessimistic but determined mood, the scientists adjourned and went back to their laboratories and campuses to think more about the problem.

Back in California, Oppenheimer pondered Lawrence's warning about "leftwandering activities." On November 12, he wrote Lawrence, telling him he was resigning from the Association of Scientific Workers. "I . . . assure you that there will be no further difficulties at any time with the A.A.S.W. . . . I doubt very much whether anyone will want to start at this time an organization which could in any way embarrass, divide or interfere with the work we have at hand. . . . So you can forget it." About three weeks later, on December 6, 1941, he attended a meeting of another leftist political group, whose mission was to aid victims of the Spanish Civil War. The meeting proved to be a depressing and dreary affair. The civil war in Spain by now had ended in the defeat of the democratically elected government. General Franco, an ally of Hitler, stood firmly in power. Oppenheimer left the meeting feeling as if he were coming to the end of something. As it happened, it was the last such meeting he would ever attend. The next day, December 7, Japanese airplanes bombed the American military base of Pearl Harbor in Hawaii and forced the United States into World War II. Within weeks, Robert Oppenheimer would be granted his wish to contribute to the American war effort.

CHAPTER 4 NOTES

p. 42   "Robert found it . . ." Peter Goodchild, *J. Robert Oppenheimer: Shatterer of Worlds*, p. 27.

p. 43   "Probably the most important . . ." Hans Bethe, "J. Robert Oppenheimer," *Biographical Memorial of the Fellows of the Royal Society of Science*, vol. 14, p. 391.

p. 45   "I became a real left-winger . . ." Robert Oppenheimer interview with *Time* magazine, 1948.

p. 45   "He was a tall . . ." Haakon Chevalier, *Oppenheimer: The Story of a Friendship*, p. 11.

p. 47   "[He] was overeducated . . ." I. I. Rabi, Robert Serber, Victor Weisskopf, Abraham Pais, and Glenn Seaborg. *Oppenheimer.*

p. 51   "I . . . assure you . . ." Alice Kimball Smith and Charles Weiner, eds., *Robert Oppenheimer: Letters and Recollections*, p. 220.

5

THE MANHATTAN PROJECT

The meeting that Robert Oppenheimer attended in Schenectady in November 1941 was the result of a long and tortured scientific and political process that began in the early 1930s, a process that clearly demonstrates the close relationship between science and politics and between scientists and the societies in which they live.

By 1930, nuclear physicists had made great strides in understanding the nature of the atom. The existence of the proton and electron had been proved, and many kinds of particles ejected from the atom, such as the alpha particle and gamma radiation, had been uncovered and explained. In spite of this impressive record of achievement, the public at large was generally uninformed and disinterested in the discoveries made by physicists. This lack of public response was probably caused by the theoretical and technical nature of physics. None of the speculations of physicists had actually promised a tangible change in the way most people had to think, act or work. Nuclear physics was seen almost as being an interesting hobby, an amusing activity that was at the edge of day-to-day society. Ordinary citizens weren't interested in it, and by and large neither were politicians nor military men.

However, very slowly, beginning in 1932, this attitude about physics began to change as a result of yet another discovery about the nucleus of atoms. In February 1932, at the Cavendish Laboratory, a British physicist, James Chadwick, happened upon still another particle jarred loose from the atomic nucleus. This latest constituent part of the nucleus was named the neutron, because it was shown to have a neutral electric charge, that is, it is neither positively nor negatively charged like the proton or the electron, respectively.

Chadwick proved the existence of neutrons in an elegant and indirect fashion typical of nuclear physics. Beginning with the elements polonium and beryllium, he placed a succession of materials in an experimental chamber. Chadwick knew that polonium was radioactive, that it emitted alpha particles, which in turn knocked other, as yet unidentified, particles out of the beryllium. Irène and Frédéric Joliot-Curie, the daughter and son-in-law of Marie Curie, had previously identified a kind of radiation coming from the nucleus of beryllium, but the Joliot-Curies believed this radiation to be gamma rays, which have high energy and are virtually weightless. Chadwick believed that these particles were in fact heavier and more substantial than gamma rays. To prove this, he positioned a layer of paraffin (which contains many hydrogen atoms) between the beryllium and a Geiger counter, which counted the number of particles that hit the far wall of the experiment container. Chadwick set up an intricate cause-and-effect chamber: first the alpha particle from the polonium knocked loose the unidentified particle from the beryllium; then, he speculated, the unidentified particle from the beryllium would in turn knock loose a particle from the hydrogen in the paraffin. This last particle would be measured by the Geiger counter and by a series of aluminum sheets that Chadwick would eventually set between the paraffin and Geiger counter.

At the beginning of the experiment, the Geiger counter fluctuated and sounded wildly as it recorded a high number of particle hits. Then, one by one, Chadwick placed the thin aluminum strips between the paraffin and the Geiger counter until finally he recorded no particles hitting the counter at all. The density of enough aluminum strips had finally stopped all of the particles from hitting the back wall. By measuring the distance between these strips compared to the decreasing number of hits recorded by the Geiger counter, Chadwick calculated that the particles being knocked loose from the paraffin and registering on the Geiger counter were protons.

The fact that they were protons was important because it disproved the Joliot-Curies' theory that the radiation from the beryllium, which knocked the protons from the paraffin loose, was gamma rays. Weightless gamma rays could not knock a heavyweight proton loose from its atom. This would be like throwing a pool ball against a boulder and expecting the boulder in turn to be thrown a mile from its resting place. The pool ball simply wouldn't be big enough to accomplish this. However, another boulder, if it were moving fast enough and encountered no interference, could do this.

Also Chadwick used mathematics to prove that the particles from the beryllium had to have no electrical charge in order to penetrate the strong positive charge created by the protons in the atomic nucleus of the paraffin. If the beryllium particle had an electrical charge, it would encounter electromagnetic interference once it approached the atomic nucleus. Because of the power of its impact, the particle coming from the beryllium and knocking a proton out of the paraffin had to be neutrally charged and possess a similar weight as the proton—thus, it was a neutron. Because of its weight and especially its great penetrating power, the neutron became very useful in experimental physics.

In the first month of the next year, 1933, an event in the world of politics occurred in Germany that would soon have grave

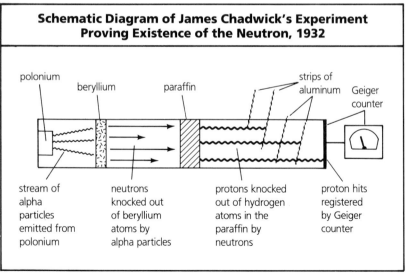

Schematic Diagram of James Chadwick's Experiment Proving Existence of the Neutron, 1932

Figure 4

repercussions on science and scientists around the world. That month, Adolf Hitler came to power in Germany. Quickly, Hitler silenced opposition to himself and his party, the National Socialist (or Nazi) Party, in Germany and imprisoned anyone who dared speak out against him. Then he began to reorganize German universities and scientific institutions, harassing, demoting and even jailing scientists whose personal beliefs or ethnic origins did not correspond to those of the Nazi Party. Singled out for punishment were Jewish scientists.

Because of this punishment, many prominent German scientists of Jewish origin left Germany over the next five years. This was an impressive group, among whom probably the most impressive figure was Albert Einstein, at that time considered the premier physicist in the world. Besides Einstein, however, a number of excellent, but lesser-known scientists also were forced to flee Germany. Many of these people later worked with Robert Oppenheimer on the American nuclear bomb project or sat out the war in neutral European countries such as Sweden.

One of these scientists was the physicist Lise Meitner, who was forced to leave Germany in 1937. From her exile in Sweden, Meitner worked by mail with her long-time colleague Otto Hahn on a problem that eventually proved to be of great interest and importance to governments throughout the world. In 1938, Hahn, who was a chemist, studied the properties of uranium that had been bombarded with James Chadwick's newly discovered neutrons. Hahn had expected to find that the neutrons had caused a mild atomic rearrangement in the uranium and that parts of the uranium had deteriorated into radium. This sort of finding, which indicated that the neutrons had knocked out a few alpha particles from the uranium, would be consistent with the known properties of uranium at the time. Instead, Hahn was surprised to find in his uranium sample significant traces of barium, which was much lighter than either radium or uranium.

Puzzling over these experimental results, Hahn sent his data to Meitner to seek her help in theoretical interpretation. At first, Meitner was also perplexed. The presence of barium seemed to be impossible from what was known about atomic nuclei and the properties of uranium. Soon, though, Meitner was struck by a realization: The uranium was not simply decaying into isotopes (as Ernest Rutherford had shown in 1907), but it had been split almost in two by the neutrons hitting it, creating barium, lanthanum and cerium as by-products of the split. Of these elements, barium offered the most important clue because it was the most common element found and it was about half the weight of the original uranium.

Besides the astonishing fact that uranium actually split and created new elements was the even more astonishing realization that a great deal of energy, called binding energy, that held the nucleus together was released by this split. Meitner, and then other scientists in America and Germany, easily came to the calculations: In each *atom* of uranium 200 million volts of energy were released by an atomic split, or fission. For a single atom, this was an astonishing figure.

Within days, the news of fission had spread to Robert Oppenheimer in California. "This U business is unbelievable," he told a colleague. "We first saw it in the papers, wired for more dope, and have had a lot of reports since. . . . I think it is exciting, not in [a] rare way . . . but in a good honest practical way." Later, he reconsidered how "good" the discovery was to be. A small bit of uranium, he wrote another colleague, "might very well blow itself to hell."

By chance, the renowned Danish physicist Niels Bohr was visiting New York at the time that Meitner and Hahn discovered fission in uranium. For some time, Bohr had been a strong opponent of the Nazi government in Germany. He had used his influence to help many German scientists escape from Germany and had given several of them jobs at the prestigious institute for the study of physics that he headed in Copenhagen. Bohr was in the United States to deliver talks at several conferences about nuclear physics. He also informally discussed the political situation in Europe and arranged for European refugee scientists to come to universities in the United States.

Like all of his colleagues in America, Bohr immediately understood the implications of fission: It was now, in theory at least, possible to make an enormously powerful bomb out of uranium. The practical details of doing this, however, were so complicated that Bohr imagined the actual construction of the bomb would be virtually impossible. As a consequence, he didn't give much thought to the enterprise. What truly puzzled and interested Bohr was the way uranium split in half. For a long time, he had held the idea that the atomic nucleus was similar in many ways to a liquid drop. Bohr believed that the atomic nucleus was like a drop of water in that both were wobbly bundles of mass and energy held together by internal tension. Now that he knew that the drop could actually be split, he visualized this process as one similar to the way a drop of water might split. With added weight from an outside source (a neutron), the drop, or nucleus, became too heavy and unstable. Bohr imagined that, like a drop of water, the nucleus then elongated until it separated into two parts. Scientists in Denmark and the United States had also noticed a peculiarity about uranium: It appeared to fission, or split, only when the neutrons that hit it were traveling at certain speeds. Slow-moving and fast-moving neutrons seemed to split it, but uranium would not fission as often when hit by neutrons whose speeds were in between. Also, fast-moving neutrons split more of the atoms in a uranium sample than did slow-moving neutrons. Bohr immediately concentrated on trying to explain why this occurred.

Bohr knew that uranium was composed of two different isotopes, U-238 and U-235. All uranium atoms must have the same number of protons, 92. But slight variations in kinds of uranium exist because of the number of neutrons attached to the protons in the atomic nucleus. Uranium 238, for instance, has 92 protons and 146 neutrons; Uranium 235 has 92 protons and 143 neutrons. The total number of protons plus neutrons is called the mass number. Bohr was aware that uranium ore consisted of more than 99 percent U-238; U-235 accounted for only 0.7 percent. This mixture of U-235 and U-238, he reasoned, must somehow account for the way uranium split when it was hit by fast and slow neutrons. Bohr had pondered this problem for several days when a moment of inspiration came to him at Princeton University. In the middle of a conversation with another physicist, he suddenly stopped talking and rushed to an office he had borrowed from Albert Einstein. There he scribbled his thoughts down on paper; once he felt secure that he had captured his inspiration for good, he began to explain.

The fast-moving neutrons split the U-238, and both fast- and slow-moving neutrons split U-235. Later Bohr and others were to discover that U-235, because it became an even-numbered isotope of mass number 236 after it absorbed a penetrating neutron, was more prone to split than U-238, whose mass number changed to an odd number after the absorption of a neutron. In this manner, because it was likely to split from almost any neutron that hit it, the rare isotope U-235 became the material on which scientists and military men would fix their attention in their quest for a nuclear bomb. Simply put, U-235 would produce a far greater explosion than the more common U-238 because much more of it fissioned, releasing more of its binding energy.

American scientists, led by a handful of refugee physicists who had come to America to escape Nazi repression, now began to press the U.S. government for funds with which to carry out research on uranium. At this point, most of the active scheming and research for bomb-making had been carried out at Columbia and Princeton Universities in New York City and nearby New Jersey. The main participants, besides Bohr, who would only stay in the United States for a few months, were Enrico Fermi, Leo Szilard, Edward Teller and Eugene Wigner. All were refugees; Fermi had fled Italy to protect his Jewish wife from the ravages of Italian fascism; Szilard, Teller and Wigner were Hungarians who had fled Europe to escape the Nazi war machine.

In March 1939, just three months after Bohr's illumination about the differences between U-235 and U-238, the first group of American scientists met with a representative of the U.S. Navy. Fermi, because he was a Nobel Prize winner, was sent by the New York group to talk with the navy. Fermi detailed the discoveries that had been made in the past year and explained how such breakthroughs could be used to build a superbomb. He emphasized that many technical problems remained to be solved before the bomb could be built and requested funding from the government to help solve these. He also emphasized that the problem was an urgent one. The community of scientists was like a country with no boundaries; whatever scientists in America could figure out about uranium could also eventually be discovered by scientists in other countries. Whether it wanted to admit it or not, Fermi argued, the

U.S. government was now in a race with the German government to develop the atomic bomb. The naval committee headed
by Admiral Stanford Hooper, was not enthusiastic about Fermi's
request. The project seemed too fantastic and the details too
fuzzy for their taste. Hooper committed no money but said that
the navy would stay in touch, a weak response that disappointed
Fermi.

Meanwhile, back in New York, Szilard and others urged Niels
Bohr not to publish a paper containing the results of his calculations about uranium. The information, they said, was too
important to be made public. Nazi scientists and government
officials would immediately understand the implications of
Bohr's work and begin to work on the bomb themselves. Even
though he hated the Nazi regime, Bohr argued that he could not
keep the information secret. Scientists, Bohr believed, belonged
to an open, international community whose membership went
beyond national borders. Science, Bohr said, only worked when
everyone submitted the results of his or her labors openly to the
criticism and scrutiny of others. This had been a tradition in
science at least since the 18th century, when the openness of the
Enlightenment replaced the secrecy of earlier scientific tradition. Bohr insisted that withholding information would slow
progress in science and create an atmosphere of paranoia and
distrust that benefited no one.

Bohr and the others continued their debate until March 18, when
a paper by the Joliot-Curies, who had continued to study the
properties of uranium, appeared in the English scientific journal
Nature. In their paper, the Joliot-Curies discussed much of the
same information that Bohr had speculated about. With the Joliot-
Curie paper, the genie of uranium had now been let out of its bottle,
and as far as Leo Szilard and other American scientists were
concerned, the race for an atomic weapon had begun in earnest.

Szilard and his colleagues still had a long way to go to transform
uranium into an explosive weapon. The odds of achieving this, as
estimated by one scientist, were about 10 percent. Such a low
probability of success would have daunted most people, but
Szilard, Wigner and Teller were unwilling to gamble that an
atomic weapon was impossible to make. Yet, in spite of their

efforts to interest American government officials, their pleas continued to fall on deaf ears.

Having almost reached the point of despair, in July 1939 Szilard was struck with an inspiration. He would try to visit the one person whose endorsement nobody could dismiss, the renowned Nobel Prize–winning physicist Albert Einstein, whose summer residence happened to be on nearby Long Island.

On Sunday, July 30, Edward Teller picked Szilard up in Manhattan and drove him out to Einstein's comfortable estate. Szilard explained to Einstein how fission in uranium meant the possibility of a fast uncontrolled chain reaction whose energy could release an enormous amount of explosive power. Einstein was surprised. He was a pacifist and a man who dealt with large, abstract problems; undoubtedly he had not spent much time on something as earthy and blunt as the military potential of uranium. Szilard pressed his argument, noting that a large and comprehensive research effort had to be mounted soon if the United States was to beat Germany in the race for the bomb. Setting aside his usual distaste for war projects, Einstein agreed completely with Szilard's analysis, and together they drafted a letter to the one person who could most quickly achieve this goal—Franklin Roosevelt, the president of the United States. In a simple and direct style, Einstein warned Roosevelt that:

> *Some recent work . . . leads me to expect that the element uranium may be turned into a new and important source of energy in the immediate future. . . . I believe therefore that it is my duty to bring to your attention . . . that extremely powerful new bombs of a new type . . . may be constructed [using uranium].*

Szilard and Einstein then entrusted the letter to Alexander Sachs, a friend and former aide of Roosevelt. Even though he wasn't a scientist, Sachs immediately understood the importance of the bomb project. He phoned the White House and scheduled a meeting with Roosevelt for early September 1939. However, other events intervened in Roosevelt's schedule. On September 1, 1939, Germany invaded Poland. Several days later, both France and England declared war on Germany, and in turn Japan, Germany's ally in the Far East, declared war on France and England.

Alexander Sachs finally did meet Roosevelt on October 11. Sachs presented Roosevelt with the letter from Einstein, but rather than let the president simply read it, he began to tell Roosevelt a story. Once, Sachs said, an obscure and unknown inventor had offered his services to an emperor during a crucial point in a long war. The inventor told the emperor that he could build him a fleet of ships that needed no sails and which could carry his army to the homeland of the emperor's enemy. Because they were powered by engines and not dependent on sails, these ships could be depended on to ferry soldiers in every kind of weather. The emperor, believing the inventor talked a load of nonsense, turned the inventor down cold. The emperor was Napoleon; his enemy had been the British, who defeated Napoleon decisively in 1815; and the inventor was Robert Fulton, the man who later made the first steam-driven sailing vessels. With this cautionary tale as a prelude, Roosevelt listened carefully to the rest of Sachs's pitch. When Sachs had finished, Roosevelt called in his assistant, General Edwin "Pa" Watson. He handed the Einstein memorandum to Watson, saying simply, "This requires action."

The federal bureaucracy did not leap to action at Roosevelt's call, but slowly and with constant prodding by the physicists, it responded to the demands being placed on it. The first group formed to guide and assist the scientists on their quest was named the Advisory Committee on Uranium, known in short-hand as the Uranium Committee. This group was led by Lyman Briggs, a scientist who headed the government Bureau of Standards. For almost a year, the Uranium Committee, under Briggs's leadership, moved slowly. Some work was made toward building a stack of uranium bricks, known as the "pile," which would test whether natural uranium could be manipulated into a "controlled" chain reaction, that is, one that would generate a large amount of heat without actually exploding. This experiment would allow scientists to determine technical details about the bomb and also promised another, more hopeful outcome: the use of uranium to fuel power plants for the production of electricity.

Soon, mainly as a result of its slow progress, the Uranium Committee was dissolved and its duties were assumed by a new group called the National Defense Research Council, headed by Vannevar Bush, President Roosevelt's science advisor, and James Conant, also a scientist and president of Harvard University. Bush and Conant immediately began to make the difficult decisions about priorities that the Uranium Committee had been unable to come to grips with. First they assigned Enrico Fermi, with the assistance of Leo Szilard, to head the atomic pile program. Fermi was to lead a team that would build a large-scale atomic pile in association with the University of Chicago. This team, besides working on the controlled chain reaction, would try to produce inside the nuclear reactor a completely new element, number 94, eventually named plutonium, which seemed likely to fission in a similar way to U-235. The chemist Glenn Seaborg was put in charge of the project to test and extract plutonium.

In California, Ernest Lawrence was drafted to try to extract U-235 from the much more predominant U-238. Lawrence was optimistic that he could do this by using his huge cyclotrons to separate magnetically the two isotopes from each other. Lawrence, in turn, enticed Robert Oppenheimer to join the bomb effort, and Oppenheimer was soon put in charge of an informal group of theoretical physicists who worked on the actual design of the bomb itself. Last, Bush and Conant selected a day-to-day manager to oversee the rapidly growing bomb project. The man they chose was 46-year-old Colonel Leslie Groves, a hard-driving career army officer, an engineer by training, who had just completed the building of the Pentagon, the War Department headquarters in Washington. Groves was promoted to brigadier general and given almost unlimited authority to move the project forward. Groves gave the entire bomb project an intentionally misleading name, the Manhattan Project, after the original location of his office on Manhattan Island in New York City.

Grove's job was frightening in its scope. Not only was he in charge of creating a new weapon from a completely untested technology, but he also had to build an enormous system of manufacturing plants to provide the basic material—plutonium and U-235—from which the bomb would be made. This meant that, in effect, at breakneck speed he had to build a new industry from scratch, one that at the end of the war equaled the size of the entire American automobile industry.

To accomplish this task, Groves moved on all fronts at once. He discovered that the Belgian government had sent 1,250 tons of high-concentrate uranium ore to the United States from its mines in the Congo. The ore had been languishing in port at New York City for six months before Groves was appointed director of the Manhattan Project. The day after Groves was appointed, he arranged to buy the ore. On that same day, Groves also bought for the government 52,000 acres of land for uranium processing factories near Knoxville in eastern Tennessee. Finally, two weeks later, in October 1942, he came to Berkeley, California, to inspect Ernest Lawrence's cyclotrons. On this trip he met Robert Oppenheimer for the first time.

Improbably, Oppenheimer and Groves hit it off. Groves's bluff and impatient demeanor was not so different from Oppenheimer's own "beastliness." It is likely that they weighed each other carefully, each seeing a little of himself in the other. Groves, who was looking for someone to direct and oversee laboratory work on the bomb, explained the lab setup of the Manhattan Project to Oppenheimer. Initially, Groves favored the arrangement he had inherited: a system of separate labs, where the details of each lab's work could be controlled and compartmentalized. This, he felt, allowed for tighter security, which would better protect the secret work of the project's scientists. Oppenheimer, brash as usual, argued that the various laboratories scattered around the country doing work on the bomb project had to be brought together at one place. This centralization would maximize efficiency, stir creativity among the scientists, and speed the project. This idea appealed to Groves, who saw a way in this approach to solve security problems while at the same time speeding up work. Perhaps, Oppenheimer suggested, a remote lab in an isolated spot would allow the army to monitor scientists and their work more easily and protect them from spies.

Groves left Berkeley for Chicago deeply impressed with Robert Oppenheimer's leadership potential. Here was a man who not only in Groves's estimation, was a genius but who could put together and drive a team of quirky physicists toward a common goal. Oppenheimer, Groves thought, had the tremendous power of concentration to accomplish this part of the Manhattan Project. However, not all of Oppenheimer's acquaintances saw these qualities in the Berkeley scientist. "It was a real stroke of genius on Groves's part to have chosen [Oppenheimer]," one of Oppenheimer's colleagues said later. It was, he added, from the point of view of many scientists, "an improbable appointment." In the view of some of these scientists, Oppenheimer was an untested leader. Even though he had built a fine physics department at Berkeley, he had never directed or administered a laboratory or academic department before. Worst of all in the minds of some scientists, Oppenheimer lacked the Nobel Prize, the certificate of achievement that could command instant respect among the men he was likely to need in his lab.

On his arrival in Chicago, Groves immediately proposed Oppenheimer as director of the lab to a group known as the Military Policy Committee. This group was strongly influenced by members of military intelligence, who quickly discovered Oppenheimer's Communist connections. In their eyes, a man whose former fiancée, wife, brother and sister-in-law were or had been members of the Communist Party was not suitable as director of the nation's most secret military laboratory. True to form, Groves was more concerned about his own pressing timetable than Robert Oppenheimer's security problems. In mid-October, he demanded and won permission to appoint Oppenheimer director of the new, centralized lab.

Oppenheimer, moving with a speed that must have impressed Groves, made a trip in mid-November to the Southwest to begin inspecting sites for the new lab. Within days, he found a likely site. The new lab would be housed on a large mesa in north-central New Mexico. It was a place Oppenheimer knew well from his days roaming the mountains on horseback in the twenties and thirties, and it was not far from Oppenheimer's summer retreat, Perro Caliente. Los Alamos had a stunning view that to Oppenheimer was ideal for reflective thought; it combined what Robert Oppenheimer called his "two great loves—physics and desert country."

Having found his ideal spot for a nuclear laboratory, Oppenheimer now turned to face his first serious test as director of the Los Alamos Laboratory: to cajole and persuade the best minds in physics to join him there.

CHAPTER 5 NOTES

p. 57   "This U business . . ." Alice Kimball Smith and Charles Weiner, eds., *Robert Oppenheimer: Letters and Recollection*, p. 270.

p. 61   "Some recent work . . ." Phillip Frank, *Einstein: His Life and Times,* p. 89.

6

TICKLING THE DRAGON'S TAIL

On the night of February 16, 1943, by the light of a full moon six men parachuted from a lone British bomber onto a frozen lake in southern Norway. Once they landed on the ground, this well-armed commando team quickly buried their parachutes and vanished into the heavy forest that crept up to the lake's edge. The team had been sent on the direct orders of Brigadier General Leslie Groves, head of the Manhattan Project in the United States, to blow up a single, isolated factory snuggled deep in Norway's fjords and mountains.

Eleven days later, with the assistance of Norwegian underground fighters, the commando team slipped past Nazi soldiers guarding the Vemork Hydro Plant. Using plans supplied by the engineer who had designed the Vemork plant, the commandos entered the factory through an external opening in the factory's ductwork. Burrowing their way down the narrow duct deep into the bowels of the factory, they came to a series of machines that laboriously extracted a rare kind of water from the deep lake above the plant. Carefully, the guerrilla fighters attached explosive charges to each of the extraction cells and set the timers. Then they crawled back up the duct as fast as they could go. The charges went off before they had time to leave the plant, ripping open the machinery and spilling half a ton of the precious water down the pipes into the river below. As a result of the explosions, the extractor cells were so damaged that they would be out of action for several months. Most important, the manufacturing process was severely disrupted. Even after repairs, none of the precious water would be available to the plant's customers for almost a year.

The extraordinary importance of this small, obscure factory lay in the product it produced and the identity of the plant's largest client. The Vemork Hydro Plant was the only factory under Nazi control that manufactured heavy water, a rare kind of water in which the hydrogen atoms (having one proton and no neutrons) are replaced by an isotope of hydrogen called deuterium, which has one proton *and* a neutron. By 1943, the importance of heavy water had become obvious to the Allied command of Britain and the United States. In 1942, the Allies had received word that German scientists, too, were working on an atomic bomb project. Allied intelligence agents had monitored shipments of heavy water from Norway to Germany. From this information, the Allies deduced that the Nazis were conducting experiments with controlled uranium chain reactions in which heavy water was used as a moderator, or an agent to keep the nuclear reaction from running out of control. By stopping the Nazis' access to heavy water, the United States and Britain hoped to delay Germany's work on the atomic bomb.

At about the same time that the Norwegian commandos were blowing up the Vemork Hydro Plant, Robert Oppenheimer found himself immersed in selling the idea of Los Alamos to his fellow scientists. At first, General Groves had suggested, with Oppenheimer's enthusiastic support, that all scientists be enlisted as army officers in order to put them directly under a military-style chain of command. Immediately, the scientists whom Oppenheimer had visited on his recruiting trips rebelled against this idea. I. I. Rabi, a physicist from Columbia University, told Oppenheimer that scientists would never give up their scientific freedom to any army command. Oppenheimer relayed this and other complaints to General Groves, who quickly compromised. The scientists would be hired as civilian employees of the War Department, but security at the Los Alamos site would be enforced by the army, and Oppenheimer, as the lab's director, would have authority to hire and fire scientists and technicians in consultation with the lab's security officer.

A certain irony was attached to Groves's delegation to Oppenheimer of security matters at Los Alamos because Oppenheimer himself was still under intense scrutiny by members of the army intelligence team. Three intelligence officers in particular had their eyes on the director of the Los Alamos Lab. Colonel John Lansdale, an aide to General Groves, was the officer in charge of overall security for the Manhattan Project. Lansdale had been shown the FBI's extensive file on Oppenheimer, a dossier that confirmed the Communist Party membership of Frank Oppenheimer and others, and Robert Oppenheimer's prewar involvement in organizations that the FBI believed were controlled by the Communist Party. Lansdale was suspicious of Oppenheimer but gradually came to the conclusion from long conversations with Oppenheimer and his wife, Kitty, that the lab director would never pass information to agents of the Nazi government and was unlikely to pass information to the Soviet Union.

On the West Coast, Colonel Boris Pash, the army officer in charge of intelligence for that region, harbored a more distrustful view of Oppenheimer. From telephone taps of Communist Party offices in San Francisco and surveillance of several of Oppenheimer's former students, Pash believed that a Communist espionage "cell" was operating in Ernest Lawrence's cyclotron laboratories. Furthermore, he felt that this cell was in some way tied to Oppenheimer. This impression was communicated to Lansdale and the security commander at Los Alamos, Captain Peer de Silva. De Silva immediately placed Oppenheimer under tight surveillance at Los Alamos. Oppenheimer's telephone was tapped; all of his mail was opened; and agents, semidisguised as bodyguards, were assigned to watch him at all times. This treatment continued throughout the war.

Oppenheimer managed fairly well to ignore this intrusion on his privacy. In any event, he had his hands full with other pressing chores. First he recruited several of his current and former students. Robert Serber began work on the theory that would underpin bomb construction, as did Philip Morrison and David Hawkins, two other Berkeley associates. Interestingly, even though army intelligence officers now combed the files and pried into the lives of everyone coming to work at Los Alamos, they somehow missed Morrison and Hawkins's former membership in the Communist Party. Two other former students of Oppenheimer were less fortunate. David Bohm, a promising graduate student in physics, was rejected for employment by the Los Alamos army security officer, Peer de Silva, because de Silva suspected that Bohm was a member of the Communist Party. Another Oppenheimer student, Rossi Lomanitz, also suffered because of the suspicions of army intelligence. Lomanitz, who Oppenheimer called "an extremely talented student, conscientious, of unusual intelligence," had been tailed in Berkeley and San Francisco by army intelligence agents, who had decided that he was probably a Communist Party member, too. Even though they apparently had no firm evidence to support this conclusion, and even though membership in the party by itself did not mean that Lomanitz would have been disloyal to his country, army intelligence secretly began proceedings to remove him completely from wartime military scientific work. On July 30, 1943, Lomanitz, who had been working on cyclotrons with Ernest Lawrence, was unexpectedly called up for active duty in the army. He appealed this decision, but his plea was rejected personally by draft board director Lewis Hershey. Within months, Lomanitz was serving at the rank of private as a clerk in the army, a position he held throughout the war.

After recruiting former students and other lower-ranking scientists, Oppenheimer now used all of his considerable charm and persuasion to corral the senior men and women he wanted for the project. Two key players, the theoretical physicists Hans Bethe and Edward Teller, agreed quickly to join him in Los Alamos. Oppenheimer placed Bethe in charge of the Theoretical Division, a move that angered Teller because Teller sought this job himself. To placate Teller, Oppenheimer appointed him as leader of a group planning an even larger version of the bomb, a "thermonuclear" bomb that would attempt to derive its power from fusing atoms together rather than splitting them apart. Teller had decided on deuterium, the same heavy form of hydrogen manufactured in the Norwegian plant destroyed by Allied soldiers, as the principal fuel for the thermonuclear bomb. Thus the thermonuclear weapon acquired a shorthand nickname; it would commonly be known as the hydrogen bomb. Teller referred to the bomb as the "Super" because of the enormous power it promised to pack. Oppenheimer made it clear, however, that work on the fission bomb had priority over the Super.

I. I. Rabi, a physicist whom Oppenheimer desperately wanted, declined the invitation, stating he had his hands full of work on radar and noting that it would be a tragedy to waste three centuries of physics on building such a terrible weapon as the atomic bomb. Leo Szilard also declined to come to Los Alamos, although his reason for rejecting Oppenheimer had more to do with the primitive physical conditions at the desert site than moral considerations. "Nobody could think straight in a place like that," he said. "Everybody who goes there will go crazy." These rejections were disheartening to Oppenheimer, but he won an important commitment when Enrico Fermi promised to come as soon as his work on the uranium pile in Chicago was finished.

New residents arriving in Los Alamos in 1943 found the town in a state of barely controlled chaos. The old Los Alamos Ranch

Los Alamos, 1942. (Los Alamos National Laboratory)

School consisted of only 27 small houses, along with a main hall, called Fuller Lodge. Originally, in January 1943, Oppenheimer and Groves had hoped that Los Alamos would be home to around 30 scientists. Very soon, they realized this number was a gross underestimation. Groves commandeered army and local construction crews and began to build cheap, barracks-style housing and a decent road up the mesa from Santa Fe. These efforts progressed slowly, and throughout the war, conditions at Los Alamos remained primitive. The streets of the town turned into muddy troughs after rainstorms; the housing was cold in the winter, hot in the summer; there was scarcely enough water, so baths were infrequent; the entire site had only three telephones, all of which were tapped (Robert Oppenheimer had one to himself and calls were carefully restricted by military police on the other two). In spite of these difficulties, volunteers began to pour into the isolated site. By July 1943, 250 scientists, technicians, and soldiers lived and worked in Los Alamos; by the time the first bomb was tested two years later, the population of the town had swollen to more than 3,000.

"The notion of disappearing into the desert for an indeterminate period and under quasi-military auspices disturbed a good many scientists and the families of many more," Oppenheimer noted dryly. More disturbing to others, especially to recent European refugee scientists, was the high barbed-wire fence that had been strung up around the town. Laura Fermi, Enrico Fermi's wife, shared this view. "Several of the European-born were unhappy," she said, "because living inside a fence reminded them of concentration camps." In any event, by the summer of 1943, Oppenheimer and Groves had managed to establish Los Alamos as a 20th-century version of a western frontier town.

In the first seven or eight months of 1943, Oppenheimer made many trips back and forth between California and New Mexico as he recruited scientists and moved equipment from Berkeley to Los Alamos. During two of these visits, he had encounters that would come back to haunt him later.

The first of these involved his friend and fellow professor, Haakon Chevalier. In late January 1943, the Oppenheimers invited the Chevaliers over to Eagle Hill, their house in Berkeley, for dinner and drinks. At some point in the evening, Haakon Chevalier took Oppenheimer aside to mention a curious brush that Chevalier had recently had with George Eltenton, a British chemical engineer who worked in San Francisco for the Shell Oil Company. Both Oppenheimer and Chevalier knew Eltenton because of Eltenton's union activity in the Bay area. Chevalier said that Eltenton had told him that a member of the diplomatic corps at the Soviet Union's consulate in San Francisco had expressed "concern" that Soviets were being left in the dark about secret United States weapons projects. This diplomat had asked Eltenton to ask around about such information among his friends and associates. Eltenton had then asked Chevalier if he could ask Oppenheimer about the sort of work the physicist was engaged in. At Eagle Hill that evening, Chevalier apparently did not directly ask Oppenheimer for information; instead, according to Oppenheimer, he merely warned Oppenheimer about Eltenton's probes. Recalling this incident later, Oppenheimer professed shock at being asked to spy against his country. Yet, at the time, he said nothing to army intelligence officers about the incident. He finally mentioned Eltenton, but not Chevalier or Chevalier's apparent veiled attempt at getting information, to army intelligence in August 1943, nine months later.

In June 1943 Oppenheimer visited his former fiancée, Jean Tatlock, during a weekend trip to Berkeley. According to army intelligence, whose men tailed Oppenheimer around town, the physicist spent the night with Tatlock. Because Tatlock was known to be deeply involved in Communist Party politics, this episode further alarmed Colonel Pash in California. Taken together, the Tatlock episode and Oppenheimer's mention in August about the Eltenton incident incited Pash to write Colonel Lansdale that Oppenheimer should be "completely removed from the project and dismissed from employment by the United States government." Again, General Groves dismissed this advice. Oppenheimer would remain in charge of the bomb project. He was, in Groves's view, the only man for the job. Without him, the project might fail, and Groves was a man who refused to countenance failure.

In late September 1943 yet another European refugee scientist, perhaps one of the greatest of all, began his trek to America. After his visit to the United States in 1939, Niels Bohr had returned to Denmark to continue work on physics at the scientific institute he headed in Copenhagen. He had been home only about six months when the German army invaded and occupied his country. For the next three years, Bohr continued his day-to-day work in physics while secretly participating in activities of the Danish underground. Among other things, Bohr helped to hide Danish Jews from the Nazis and served as an informant to the Allies about German scientific and military plans.

In September 1943, German authorities in Denmark decided to crack down on public figures who, because of their fame, had previously escaped arrest. Hearing of this decision, the Swedish ambassador to Denmark warned Bohr of this crackdown on September 28; the next day Bohr and his family slipped away from secret police surveillance and boarded a small motorboat that took them across the 20-mile Øresund strait to safety in neutral Sweden. On October 6, Bohr was whisked from Sweden to England aboard a two-engine British Mosquito bomber that made a regular—and dangerous—crossing carrying diplomatic pouches. Before the flight, Bohr was given a parachute and tucked into the small bomb bay of the plane. In the event of an attack by German fighter aircraft against the Mosquito, the pilot had been instructed to open the bomb bay door and let Bohr parachute into the ocean. Presumably, if they could find him, British boats would then pluck the world-renowned physicist from the sea.

Bohr's flight proved not to be quite this dramatic, although he did lose consciousness for a while when he failed to hear the pilot's order to put on an oxygen mask. By the time the plane landed in Scotland, Bohr was alert and relieved to be on solid ground. In December 1943, the British sent Bohr to the United States as part of the Los Alamos team. Sometime around Christmas, Bohr and his son and several British scientists arrived at the isolated train stop of Lamy, high in the desert about 15 miles from Santa Fe. Bohr's arrival at Los Alamos symbolically completed the first phase of Robert Oppenheimer's ordeal in the desert. Now he and the others had to figure out how to make a bomb before the Germans did.

Research with the aim of solving the practical difficulties of bomb construction and design had begun some months before

Bohr's arrival. One of the key questions the design group asked itself was how to build the actual explosive mechanism that would ignite an atomic weapon. Several methods were proposed, and after lively debate, two were chosen as the techniques most likely to work. Both approaches relied on a crucial theoretical concept that had arisen out of the work done by Lise Meitner and Niels Bohr in 1938 and 1939, and expanded upon by Enrico Fermi, working with his atomic "pile" in Chicago in 1942.

The concept presumed the following: U-235 split in half when bombarded by neutrons. In a large mass of purified U-235, the process of fission, or splitting, ricocheted rapidly from one uranium atom to another until a chain reaction was created. This chain reaction multiplied the energy being released by the splitting of uranium atoms. The first split creates two atoms out of what had been only one. In turn, this split sends off showers of neutrons that will split four or more other atoms, which will, in turn, spew forth yet another neutron shower that will split eight or more uranium atoms. This progression occurs with lightning speed. If enough uranium is brought together in one place, the speed of the chain reaction cannot be controlled; it will multiply until an explosion occurs. The amount of uranium necessary for a runaway chain reaction resulting in an explosion is called the critical mass.

In Chicago in November 1942, Fermi and his team actually put enough uranium together in one place to achieve a controlled chain reaction, proving for the first time experimentally a characteristic of uranium that had been predicted earlier theoretically. This critical mass experiment was extremely dangerous because, without the carbon rods inserted just the right way into his uranium pile, Fermi's experiment could have run away from him. Because of the arrangement of the pile, however, this explosion would not have been a full nuclear explosion. Nonetheless such an accident would have been devastating for the Chicago area. If this had occurred, the pile would have exploded or melted, emitting a deadly barrage of radiation that not only would have killed everyone in the room but many others in a number of city blocks around the reactor site. Fortunately, Fermi was an extremely careful experimenter as well as a capable theoretician. Work on the pile proceeded smoothly, revealing many secrets about the exact workings of uranium in chain reactions.

In the meantime, Oppenheimer, Teller, Bethe, Serber and others in Los Alamos continued to work on bomb design. The initial device they came up with looked a lot like a sawed-off artillery cannon that would fire a uranium "bullet" into a hollowed-out notch in a sphere of uranium. This type of approach was called the gun method. In theory, when the uranium bullet passed through the sphere, a critical mass of uranium would be created, which would then initiate a complete nuclear explosion. One major problem with U-235 and the gun method remained: Would the uranium fission fast enough to fully complete the nuclear explosion? Also, the scientists were planning to make a nuclear weapon out of plutonium, the human-made element that would be created in the nuclear furnace of the controlled uranium pile reactors in Chicago and others like it that the army was building in Oak Ridge, Tennessee, and Hanford, Washington. Because plutonium was human-made and did not exist on Earth naturally, its atomic qualities had to be thoroughly explored.

One of the first problems the scientists tackled was the effect of stray neutrons on uranium and plutonium. Early experimental data clearly demonstrated that stray neutrons generated from the gun method could detonate a premature explosion in the bomb, or "gadget," as Oppenheimer and the others took to calling the nuclear device. If the uranium or plutonium detonated too early it would not fully explode, that is, it would come nowhere near utilizing the full power of the fission potential of the bomb.

The Los Alamos scientists suggested several ways to get around the stray neutron problem. One was to fire the U-235 bullet at a huge rate of speed, about 3,000 feet per second. This velocity would allow the bullet to join with its mate quickly enough so that stray neutrons would not be a problem. Unfortunately, no gun in the army arsenal could fire a projectile that fast, and Oppenheimer had to order his ordnance department to begin trying to construct such a gun.

One of Oppenheimer's younger physicists, Seth Neddemeyer, proposed an entirely different approach. Rather than ramming a uranium bullet into a ball of uranium to induce an explosion, why not instead try to squeeze the uranium or plutonium into a dense core by a method known as implosion. In this scheme, a tube or pipe of uranium or plutonium would be surrounded by explosive charges, all of which would go off at the same time, forcing the uranium inward until it reached critical mass. This would eliminate the random neutron problem, but as the more experienced scientists quickly pointed out, it would also create a new problem: how to uniformly squeeze the nuclear material so that it would be neatly compressed into a critical mass. If the power of the explosive charges weren't evenly distributed, then the uranium or plutonium would simply squirt out one end or the other of the pipe.

In spite of this complaint about implosion, Oppenheimer was struck by Neddemeyer's idea and encouraged him and a small team to begin at once to test whether implosion could work. During the summer and fall of 1943, the sounds of explosions could be heard reverberating through the hills and canyons around Los Alamos as Neddemeyer attempted to perfect implosion. At around

Theoretical group discussion at Los Alamos. Oppenheimer sits at center second row; Enrico Fermi is third from left, front row. (Los Alamos National Laboratory)

Gun-type Bomb, Also Known as Little Boy

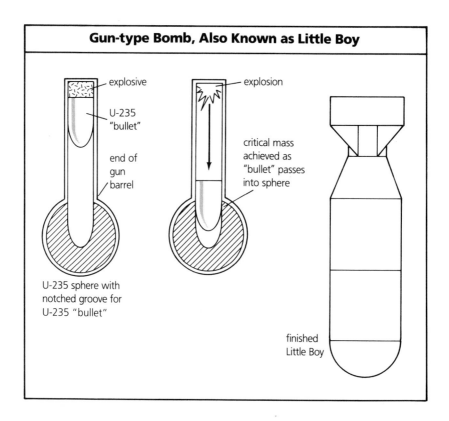

explosive

U-235 "bullet"

end of gun barrel

U-235 sphere with notched groove for U-235 "bullet"

explosion

critical mass achieved as "bullet" passes into sphere

finished Little Boy

this same time, other physicists working with a small cyclotron determined that U-235 emitted and absorbed neutrons fast enough (in less than a thousand millionth of a second) to be effective in a gun-type bomb. Also, another physicist, Emilio Segré, discovered that much of the stray neutron activity that threatened the U-235 gun bomb came from cosmic rays that had not been stopped by the earth's thin atmosphere at Los Alamos's relatively high altitude. Segré calculated that if the gun mechanism were shielded, the uranium gun bomb would work. Thus, Oppenheimer ordered a halt on the high velocity gun; a regular, modified army cannon would do. The uranium gun "gadget" seemed to be well on its way to completion.

Oppenheimer and his team could not be so sure about the success of the plutonium bomb. For one thing, they had discovered that plutonium emitted a very high number of neutrons, which meant that plutonium could not be used on the gun-type bomb. A plutonium bomb probably could work through implosion, but the experiments with implosion were not going well. By early 1944, Oppenheimer faced a difficult choice. He knew that the Manhattan Project's factories in Tennessee and Washington would probably begin delivering the first batches of U-235 and plutonium within 12 to 18 months, and that at first the U.S. government would have only enough nuclear material for a few bombs. Therefore, the scientists had to make *both* the gun-type and the implosion bomb work, and they had to begin making them work fast.

Early in 1944, Oppenheimer decided to replace Seth Neddemeyer as leader of the implosion team with George Kistiakowsky, an explosives expert brought in from the outside. This decision, one of several personnel reorganizations that Oppenheimer had to make, highlights the intense stress and emotional pressure felt by everyone working at Los Alamos. George Kistiakowsky recalled that after the war "everything . . . looked so simple, so easy, and everybody was friends with everybody." He stressed that this was not the case at Los Alamos during 1944 and 1945. "After a few weeks . . ." he said, remembering the shock of his initial reaction, "I found that my position was untenable because I was essentially in the middle trying to make sense of the efforts of two men [Seth Neddemeyer and his boss, Deke Parsons] who were at each other's throats." Throughout this period of turmoil, Oppenheimer usually maintained a sure touch as lab director. Occasionally he lost his composure and screamed or humiliated scientists who were making little headway. These incidents were unusual, however. What is truly remarkable about Oppenheimer's leadership was that it was so steady in spite of the pressures being brought to bear on him.

A major blow from the outside came early in 1944, when Oppenheimer discovered that his one-time fiancée, Jean Tatlock, had committed suicide in Berkeley. The army, which had continued to watch Tatlock, knew of her death almost immediately but did not tell Oppenheimer. When he found out about it more than a month later, he dropped his work and took a long walk through the pine forests above the mesa. Also, around this time, the isolation of living inside a fenced-in town began to wear on Kitty Oppenheimer, and she started to drink heavily. Finally, the army's surveillance of Oppenheimer, of which Oppenheimer himself was quite aware, continued unabated. In spite of the ever-increasing pressure, Oppenheimer's sure touch

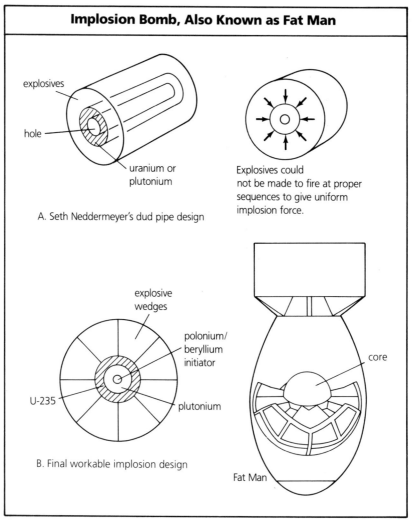

Implosion Bomb, Also Known as Fat Man

explosives

hole

uranium or plutonium

A. Seth Neddermeyer's dud pipe design

Explosives could not be made to fire at proper sequences to give uniform implosion force.

explosive wedges

polonium/ beryllium initiator

U-235

plutonium

B. Final workable implosion design

core

Fat Man

Figure 6

Saturday night dance at Fuller Lodge, Los Alamos, 1945. (Los Alamos Historical Museum Photo Archives)

allowed work to proceed steadily. "Throughout the war years," Edward Teller was to say later about Oppenheimer,

Oppie knew in detail what was going on in every part of the laboratory. He was incredibly quick and perceptive in analyzing human as well as technical problems. . . . Oppie knew [what the staff's] relationships with one another were and what made them tick. He knew how to organize, cajole, humor, soothe feelings—how to lead powerfully without seeming to do so. He was an exemplar of dedication, a hero who never lost his humanness. Disappointing him somehow carried with it a sense of wrongdoing.

Oppenheimer began to get positive results beginning late in 1944 and 1945. The first good news came with implosion. Before his stay at Los Alamos, Kistiakowsky had conducted extensive research with fast- and slow-burning explosives. Because of this experience, he knew that explosives could be molded into precise instruments, yielding intense power in a controlled way. Utilizing his knowledge, Kistiakowsky rearranged the configuration of the implosion bomb. Instead of being contained in a pipelike device, it would now be shaped like a sphere. The explosives, a combination of fast- and slow-burning types, would be arranged in slices around the central atomic core and fired precisely so that an exact shock wave would be blown inward, compressing the plutonium into a critical mass. Test results throughout 1944 began to indicate that this approach would work.

Early in 1945, the last of the major experiments testing various mock-ups of the bomb began. Perhaps the most important and dangerous of these were the experiments to simulate the milliseconds during which a chain reaction runs wild, causing a nuclear explosion. Otto Frisch, yet another of Los Alamos's refugee scientists, directed this effort. Frisch built a small pile of uranium bricks on top of a table. Above the table, he constructed two aluminum railings that held a two-by-six-inch slug of uranium. Frisch and his team dropped the slug through a hole in the uranium pile and measured the nuclear reaction resulting from the contact between the two. The uranium he used was much more purified than normal, but not quite as purified as that of the real bomb. Nonetheless, as Frisch explained:

> It was as near as we could possibly go towards starting an atomic explosion without actually being blown up, and the results were most satisfactory. Everything happened exactly as it should. When the core dropped through the hole we got a large burst of neutrons and a temperature rise of several degrees in that very short split second during which the chain reaction proceeded as a sort of a stifled explosion.

One of Frisch's co-workers nicknamed this technique "tickling the dragon's tail." From this and other work, Oppenheimer's team was able to determine that approximately 15 kilograms (about 33 pounds) of uranium or 5 kilograms (about 12 pounds) of plutonium would be needed for the core of the bomb. This small hunk of metal converted into an unbelievable amount of power, as Oppenheimer soon found out at Trinity. A few days after the explosion of the first nuclear bomb in the New Mexico desert, American scientists calculated the force of the blast. The 5 kilograms of plutonium in

Robert Oppenheimer and General Leslie Groves at remains of Trinity site tower several days after nuclear explosion. (UPI/Bettmann)

the Trinity bomb yielded an explosion that was the equivalent of 18.5 kilotons of dynamite, that is, 18,500 tons, or 370,000 pounds of dynamite. This was more than any of the scientists had expected. It would be enough to destroy an entire city.

CHAPTER 6 NOTES

p. 79   "everything . . . looked so simple . . ." Peter Goodchild, *J. Robert Oppenheimer: Shatterer of Worlds*, p. 112.

p. 81   Oppie knew in detail . . ." Richard Rhodes, *The Making of the Atomic Bomb*, p. 539.

p. 82   "It was as near as . . ." Otto Frisch, *What Little I Remember*, p. 159.

7

HIROSHIMA

The project to build the atomic bomb was conceived in 1939 as a response to fears that Nazi Germany had already begun work on a bomb of its own. Yet, ironically, the Nazi government surrendered to the Allies on May 8, 1945 (a little more than two months before the United States tested its first atomic weapon) without having come near achieving its goal.

The high command of the U.S. Army did not know until relatively late in the war exactly how far the Germans were from making an atomic weapon. The first in-depth look at German efforts came only after the Allied invasion of France in June 1944. At that time, General Groves sent to Europe a team whose mission was to ferret out as much as it could about German atomic secrets. This group, code-named the Alsos mission (*Alsos* is the Greek word for "groves," a reference to General Groves), was headed by Boris Pash (the same security officer who had given Robert Oppenheimer such a hard time in California) and an old friend of Oppenheimer, the physicist Samuel Goudsmit.

The Alsos team found almost nothing to help them with their assessment of German atomic work until it entered Strasbourg, a city that lies on the Rhine River at Germany's border with France, in November 1944, hours after Allied troops captured the town. With German artillery shells occasionally exploding around them, Pash and Goudsmit began to interrogate a number of scientists who had been captured at a local hospital, where they had tried to pass themselves off as medical doctors. None of the captured scientists cooperated, but fortunately, the Alsos team located the Germans' offices in the basement of the hospital.

As Goudsmit and his small group of scientists began going through the technical files, they discovered to their surprise that the German effort to build a bomb, after a quick and promising start in 1940, had almost completely stopped by 1942. Why this had happened was unclear at first. All the officers knew was that the Germans did not have the bomb and were unlikely to have it before they were defeated by Allied forces. Later, they discovered several factors accounting for the German failure. First, it appears that some of the German scientists, fearing the consequences of an atomic weapon in the hands of Adolf Hitler, sabotaged the project by providing false or misleading information to the German bomb team. The work of Walter Bothe provides a particularly interesting example in this regard.

In 1941, Bothe, who was a first-rate physicist and would eventually share a Nobel Prize with Max Born, Oppenheimer's former teacher in Göttingen, was assigned the task of determining if carbon was a suitable material to use as a moderator in an atomic pile. In the United States, Enrico Fermi and his group had already confirmed that carbon was a cheap and effective moderator, and they used it in their pile in Chicago. Fortunately for the Manhattan project, secrecy had been imposed just before Fermi's work with the pile, so that no scientific papers about the role of carbon had been published. Therefore, the Germans had to discover this bit of information themselves.

The problem of which moderator worked and which didn't revolved around how many neutrons the moderator absorbed. The ideal moderator slowed down the transmission of neutrons—and thus the speed of the chain reaction—without absorbing too many neutrons, which would have stopped the chain reaction completely. Not many materials had just the right atomic makeup to be used as moderators in a nuclear reactor. The Germans already knew they could use heavy water, but heavy water was scarce (their only source was the Vemork plant in Norway). Carbon was much easier to come by, but would it work? Bothe calculated that it would not work because it absorbed too many neutrons. This apparent miscalculation set the Germans back months, especially after the Allies bombed the Vemork plant in 1943. It is possible that Bothe simply made a mistake in his calculations, but it is also interesting to note that earlier in the 1930s, he had been persecuted and demoted at Heidelberg University because of his anti-Nazi politics. His mistaken calculation might have been his way of getting back at an old enemy inside his own country.

Besides possible saboteurs inside their organization, the Germans also simply did not have the visionary leadership or the economic and industrial capacity to match the United States. Hitler, who was briefed only a few times about nuclear weapons, seemed not to understand fully their power. Furthermore, the team of German scientists, led by Werner Heisenberg—yet another acquaintance of Oppenheimer's—found itself bogged down in petty bureaucratic squabbles between different government agencies, each of which wanted to control bits and pieces of the project. By late 1942, this disorganization had settled into a permanent inertia.

The Alsos team quickly relayed their hopeful findings to General Groves, who elected to share this news with only a small group of senior politicians, military men and scientists. By now, Groves instinctively withheld any information relating to atomic weaponry, fearing a leak to the Soviet Union as much or more than to Germany or Japan. Also, Groves did not want to stir up his own scientists, many of whom were motivated almost totally by a fear of Germany. If these men and women knew that Germany didn't have the bomb, Groves reckoned, they might not pursue the American bomb project with the proper zeal.

Groves had already sniffed the first breeze of dissent within the Manhattan Project's scientific community. Late in 1944, led by the restless Leo Szilard, a number of scientists who had been working on the atomic pile in Chicago signed a petition that called for a public statement by the U.S. government revealing the existence of the bomb project. This petition was deliberately misdirected by Groves through bureaucratic channels and ignored, but it revealed uneasiness about the bomb of the part of those who had worked hardest to create it.

In the view of a number of Manhattan Project scientists, several problems relating to the bomb had to be faced. The first and most immediate dilemma was a moral one: whether or not to use the bomb on Japan? Second, those who looked beyond the conflict with Germany and Japan saw that two great powers, the United

States and the Soviet Union, were beginning to emerge from the ruins of World War II. Many scientists, including Robert Oppenheimer and Niels Bohr, believed that the United States had to tell the Soviets about its work on the bomb to avoid mistrust between the two superpowers after the war and an arms race that could result from that mistrust. Finally, the most farsighted of these scientists saw that the United States would be unable to keep exclusive possession of the bomb. The scientific information underpinning the design of the bomb came mainly from the realm of physics, and it could not be kept secret. There were simply too many good physicists in the world for this to happen. Furthermore, the uranium and other raw materials from which the bomb was constructed were too widespread to be cornered by just one nation. This generalized access to science and uranium meant that the world had entered a new phase in its history. Humankind had developed a weapon of such awesome destruction that any two nations possessing it could not possibly use it against each other. To do so, would invite national suicide. Derived from this unpleasant notion was another, more hopeful one. If war between nations possessing the atomic bomb was impossible, then perhaps the idea of war itself had come to an end. Perhaps the nuclear bomb would inaugurate an unprecedented era of peace.

Niels Bohr was one of the first to understand this, and typically, this realization came to him almost as if in a dream. The dilemma—and opportunity—reduced to a simple phrase: "We are in a completely new situation that cannot be resolved by war." After his arrival in New Mexico in Christmas 1943, Bohr had ample opportunity to talk to the scientists there about his hopes. One of those with whom he spoke was Robert Oppenheimer. "Bohr at Los Alamos was marvelous," Oppenheimer remarked later.

> *[Bohr] took a lively technical interest . . . but his real function, I think for almost all of us, was not technical. [He made] the enterprise seem hopeful, when many were not free of misgiving. . . . [Bohr] was clear that one could not have effective control of . . . atomic energy without a very open world. One would have respect for individual quiet, and for the quiet process of government and management; but . . . everything that might be a threat to the security of the world would have to be open to the world.*

In late August 1944, Bohr took this message directly to President Roosevelt. Roosevelt listened carefully to Bohr's ideas, and when Bohr had finished Roosevelt declared himself to be basically in agreement with the Danish Nobel laureate. He said that after a meeting with Prime Minister Winston Churchill he would consider a request for a further meeting with Bohr, implying that Bohr might be sent as a special messenger carrying details of the U.S. nuclear project from the United States to the Soviet Union.

When Roosevelt met with Churchill three weeks later, he discovered that the British prime minister wanted nothing to do with sharing information about the bomb and was furious at Bohr for putting the idea in Roosevelt's head. Roosevelt responded to Churchill's angry counterattack by abandoning Bohr's argument. The next day Churchill fired off a letter to his science adviser in England. "The President and I," he said,

> *are much worried about Professor Bohr. How did he come into this business? He is a great advocate of publicity. . . . He says he is in close correspondence with a Russian professor. . . . The professor has urged him to go to Russia in order to discuss matters. What is this about? It seems to me Bohr ought to be confined or at any rate made to see that he is very near the edge of mortal crimes. I had not visualized this before . . . I do not like it at all.*

Bohr was not imprisoned, but his influence on Roosevelt suddenly ceased, and he would not hear from the American president again.

In March 1945, as American scientists, still believing in an imminent Nazi nuclear threat, rushed furiously to finish the bomb, American political and military planners began to decide how to use the bomb. However, before any firm decisions had been made, on April 12, 1942, President Roosevelt died of a brain hemorrhage in Warm Springs, Georgia. The new president, Harry Truman, formerly a senator from Missouri and before that an owner of a clothing store in Independence, Missouri, knew nothing of the Manhattan Project. Truman, a man of great common sense but limited formal education, lacked the charisma and enormous personal authority of Franklin Roosevelt. Because of his inexperience, Truman elected to depend heavily on the advice of Roosevelt's top aides, most of whom Truman asked to stay in their posts after Roosevelt's death. One of the most important of these assistants was Secretary of War Henry Stimson, who informed Truman about the Manhattan Project the day after Truman was sworn in as president.

Truman was thrust into the presidency at a most awkward time. American planning about strategies to end the Second World War and postwar nuclear policy had reached a critical juncture just before President Roosevelt's death, and Truman was forced to make a number of important decisions in the first weeks of his presidency. The first of these came a week and a half after Truman was sworn in, during a long meeting with General Groves and Secretary of War Stimson. At this meeting the three men decided the government needed a formal group of experts and seasoned political hands to guide it in developing nuclear policy. At Stimson's urging, Truman authorized the creation of this organization, called the Interim Committee, consisting of a mix of senior scientists and politicians, most prominently Secretary of War Stimson, the incoming Secretary of State James Byrnes, and the two senior administrators of the Manhattan Project, Vannevar Bush and James Conant. Bush and Conant, feeling uncomfortable that none of the working scientists had been brought aboard, proposed that a Scientific Panel be created to advise the Interim Board. This proposal was accepted, and Arthur Compton, Ernest Lawrence, Enrico Fermi and Robert Oppenheimer were appointed to the board.

The first full meeting of the Interim Committee with its Scientific Panel took place on May 31, 1945, almost three weeks after the surrender of Germany, which ended the war in Europe. At this meeting many of the crucial questions raised by Bohr and others were aired for debate and a number of important decisions were reached. First the committee asked Oppenheimer to brief them on the progress of the bomb project, the power of the weapon and likely follow-up projects after the war.

Oppenheimer ran down the numbers for them. The bombs on which the Los Alamos team was working were likely to have blast yields equivalent to 2,000 to 20,000 tons of dynamite. The larger hydrogen bomb, the Super, could be expected to have a yield as much as 500 times greater than that—from 10 *million* tons of TNT on up. These figures were so far beyond the comprehension of some of the civilian committee members that for a moment they lapsed into a stunned silence.

After Oppenheimer finished his briefing, the subject of sharing information with the Russians and others was reviewed. According to notes made during the meeting, Oppenheimer opened this subject by observing:

> [Even though] the immediate concern [of the bomb project] had been to shorten the war . . . it [would be] wise for the United States to offer to the world free interchange of information with particular emphasis on the development of peace-time uses. The basic goal of all endeavors in the field should be the enlargement of human welfare. If we offer to exchange information before the bomb was actually used, our moral position would be greatly strengthened.

Most of the others instinctively disliked the idea of sharing information. However, Oppenheimer won a surprising ally to his argument in the person of General George Marshall, U.S. Army chief of staff. Marshall was especially concerned about postwar cooperation with the Soviets. To allay the Russians' fears, he suggested inviting several Russian scientists to witness the test at Trinity, scheduled for later in the summer. The new secretary of state, James Byrnes, quickly shot down this proposal and suggested that the United States move ahead with a permanent installation of nuclear weapons plants and research programs, while at the same time attempting to better its relations with the Soviet Union. At this point, Oppenheimer fell silent while the others shifted to Byrnes's position. The idea of negotiation and openness with the Soviets had failed, and Robert Oppenheimer, perhaps because he had felt for the first time the comforting glow of power, of being at the very top of the American governmental élite, had only weakly attempted an argument in favor of it. From that moment on, the United States embarked on a futile attempt to keep the bomb to itself.

The committee next turned to the more immediate matter of Japan. The argument for using the bomb against Japan rested on the assumption that the use of nuclear weapons against Japanese cities would break the will of the Japanese people and the military clique who controlled the Japanese war machine. In early April, Groves had stated to President Truman that the only alternative to using the bomb against Japan would be an invasion of Japan itself, an operation that Groves insisted could cost the American army as many as 1 million lives. Groves or someone else mentioned the 1 million figure at the Interim Committee meeting and was met with a rebuke from General Marshall, who thought American losses would likely be much smaller, perhaps as few as 35,000.

Apparently, to the other members, including Robert Oppenheimer, even these losses were too much. The argument now shifted to which targets to attack. General Groves had already formed a military target committee to pick possible sites for an American nuclear strike. Groves had instructed this committee that targets

> *should be places the bombing of which would most adversely affect the will of the Japanese people to continue the war. Beyond that, they should be military in nature, consisting either of important headquarters or troop concentrations, or centers of production of military equipment or supplies.*

Groves added one other chilling stipulation: "To enable us to assess accurately the effects of the bomb, the targets should not have been previously damaged by air raids." Obviously, the strike was to be an experiment in death and destruction on a grand scale. After deliberating for several weeks, the target committee suggested several sites, including the ancient city of Kyoto, Japan's former capital; Hiroshima, which hosted an army depot; the important port city of Yokohama; and two other small cities.

Even though these places had been chosen as likely targets of a nuclear attack, the final decision of whether to strike had not been made. Only President Truman could make such a major decision as that, but the Interim Committee's recommendations would play a large role in swaying Truman one way or the other. One of the committee members suggested the idea of a "demonstration" of the nuclear bomb. This plan called for a display of the bomb's power to Japanese political and military leaders at a safe place away from populated areas rather than an unannounced attack against a Japanese city. But this scheme was quickly batted down on the advice, surprisingly, of Robert Oppenheimer, who pointed out that the Japanese military men might not be swayed

JAPAN

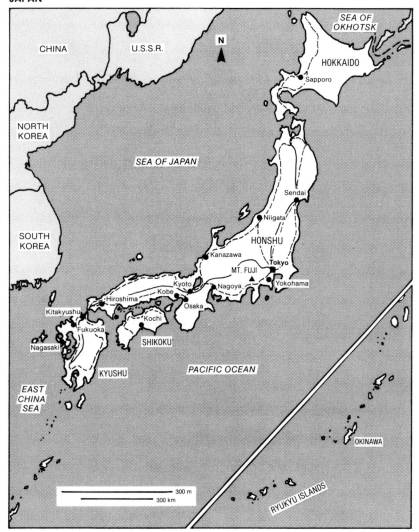

Figure 7: Major cities and islands of Japan (in 1945, North and South Korea, shown on this contemporary map, did not exist; both were occupied by the Japanese army). (© 1988 Martin Greenwald Associates, Inc.)

by a demonstration, in which case the psychological edge of surprise and shock would be lost. It was also noted that there was some chance that the bomb might not work, or that the Japanese might try to trick the Americans by moving Allied prisoners of war to the test site.

After further discussion, Secretary of State Byrnes, who was emerging as the most forceful advocate of using the bomb against Japan and for American military superiority after the war, called for a show of hands for three conclusions: (1) that the "gadget," as the scientists called it, be used against Japan; (2) that "the most desirable target would be a vital war plant . . . *closely surrounded by workers' houses";* and (3) that the Japanese not be given any prior warning about the attack. These recommendations were approved by a wide margin that included the director of the Los Alamos Laboratory. Secretary of State Byrnes relayed the recommendations of the Interim Committee to President Truman later in the week. The president, according to Stimson, "could think of no alternative and found himself in accord with what . . . the Committee [recommended]."

Back at Los Alamos, Oppenheimer plunged into the nonstop preparations for the atomic test at Trinity. Oppenheimer and his team of scientists never had much doubt that Little Boy, the gun-type bomb, would work. It would probably not be as powerful as Fat Man, as the implosion bomb had been named, but the mechanics of the firing process were much simpler and seemed assured of working. Thus, within hours after the successful test of Fat Man at Trinity on July 16, parts of the Little Boy bomb were loaded aboard the cruiser *Indianapolis* in San Francisco Bay. That evening, the ship slipped out to sea bound for Tinian Island, the most forward air base for the American bombers that had been pounding Japanese cities with conventional explosives since early in 1945.

By early August the rest of the Little Boy bomb, plus the first parts of the Fat Man bomb, had arrived via air force transport planes from New Mexico. Little Boy was assembled and armed to fire. It would be carried by a specially modified B-29 bomber and dropped over Hiroshima, the unfortunate city chosen by the Interim Committee's target group.

Before dawn on August 6, 1945, a single B-29 took off from the air base at Tinian Island. Straining under the weight of its four-ton cargo, the plane, named by its crew the *Enola Gay*, lumbered off the runway as it slowly gained enough airspeed to fly. By eight o'clock in the morning it had reached Hiroshima, a city of some 400,000 people at the mouth of the Ota River.

Hiroshima was, to a limited degree, a military target. The headquarters of Japan's Second Army Corps, the group that would lead any fight against U.S. invasion forces, was located there, as were sizable military storage depots. By 1945, large conventional bombing raids (where massed formations of Allied bombers had dumped tons of high-explosive bombs) had gutted Tokyo and other Japanese cities. Military authorities in Hiroshima, in anticipation of such a raid, had ordered the city partially evacuated. Yet, strangely, the bombers had not yet come. Nonetheless, by August, Hiroshima's population had been somewhat reduced, probably to around 300,000, the vast majority of whom were civilians.

For days, the crew of the *Enola Gay* had carefully studied maps of Hiroshima, so the pilot knew where he had to go to drop Little Boy. The single bomber probably caused no great alarm in the city. Near the outskirts of Hiroshima, the B-29 banked and headed for downtown. As it passed over the Aioi Bridge, which spanned the Ota River, a single bomb dropped from the plane's hold.

Free from the bomb's weight, the *Enola Gay* shot up into the sky after Little Boy was released. The pilot gave full throttle to the engines and dived sharply to put as much distance as possible between the aircraft and the center of town before the bomb exploded. Perhaps a minute later, the "gadget" blew. A blinding flash erupted from Hiroshima's center, and two strong shock waves shook the *Enola Gay*. As the blast spread out to form a mushroom cloud, the crew looked back in awe at what remained of the city. "I don't believe anyone ever expected to look at a sight quite like that," one of them said later. "Where we had seen a clear city two minutes before, we could now no longer see the city. We could see smoke and fire creeping up the sides of the mountains."

Below, the viewpoint was different. These are some of the accounts of the survivors:

> *Ah, that instant! I felt as though I had been struck on the back with something like a big hammer, and thrown into boiling oil. . . . I seem to have been blown a good way to the north, and I felt as though the directions were all changed around.*

"I heard a girl's voice clearly from a tree behind me," another witness recalled, "'Help me, please.' Her back was completely burned and the skin peeled off and was hanging down from her hips."

Another said: "The world seemed dark, dark all over. . . . Then I thought, 'The world is ending.'"

The blast ripped through the city, instantly destroying 70,000 buildings, 90% of the structures in the city. Forty-five thousand buildings in the city were *completely* leveled. A flash of heat in excess of 3,000°F and lasting as long as 10 to 15 seconds roasted everything within a half-mile of the Aioi Bridge, turning humans into charred, steaming balls of flesh. Over 100,000 of the city's inhabitants died instantly or during the first several days. Probably another 100,000 died of the effects of radiation poisoning within the next five years.

Back in the United States, the news of the bombing of Hiroshima was greeted with a mixture of relief, pride, joy, shock and sadness. Otto Frisch, the young physicist who only a few months before had "tickled the dragon's tail" in the canyons around Los Alamos, remembered that "one day, some three weeks after [Trinity], there was a sudden noise in the laboratory, of running footsteps and yelling voices. Someone opened my door and shouted, 'Hiroshima has been destroyed!' I remember a feeling of unease, indeed nausea, when I saw how many of my friends were rushing to the telephone to book tables at the La Fonda Hotel in Santa Fe, in order to celebrate."

Later in the day Robert Oppenheimer, the one man who more than any other had helped with the birthing of the bomb, called his team together to formally announce the news. Jubilant, Oppenheimer, in the words of one of his co-workers, "entered the room like a prize fighter. As he walked through the hall there were cheers and shouts and applause all round, and he acknowledged them with a fighter's salute—clasping his hands together above his head as he came to the podium." In the heat of the moment, Robert Oppenheimer had tasted power and felt elation. Yet, Oppenheimer was a complicated man, one who could not simply exult in success and victory. In the name of his beloved physics, Oppenheimer had created a monstrous weapon. Soon the full implications of his labors would settle in to haunt him.

In spite of the horrifying results of the Hiroshima bombing, the Japanese high command refused to allow Hirohito, the Japanese emperor, to surrender. As a result, on August 9 the American Air Force dropped another bomb, this one an implosion type like the one exploded at Trinity, on the southern city of Nagasaki. As with Hiroshima, the blast devastated Nagasaki, killing almost 100,000 more people. This blow finally proved too much for Emperor Hirohito, who five days later delivered a radio address to his people. Because his daily routine was deliberately veiled in mystery behind the walls of the imperial palace in Tokyo, few Japanese had ever heard Hirohito speak. In a thin, reedy voice he read from a prepared script:

> *Despite the best that has been done by everyone . . . the war situation has developed not necessarily to Japan's advantage. . . . Moreover, the enemy has begun to employ a new and most cruel bomb, the power of which to do damage is indeed incalculable, taking the toll of many innocent lives. . . . This is the reason we have ordered the acceptance of [the Allies' terms of surrender].*

The war was over, but for Robert Oppenheimer the struggle for power had just begun.

CHAPTER 7 NOTES

p. 88   "Bohr at Los Alamos . . ." Richard Rhodes, *The Making of the Atomic Bomb*, p. 524.

p. 89   "The president and I . . ." Ronald Clark, *The Greatest Power on Earth*, p. 177.

p. 91   "the immediate concern . . ." Richard Rhodes, *The Making of the Atomic Bomb*, p. 644.

p. 96   "Ah, that instant . . ." Arata Osata, *Children of the A-Bomb*, p. 352.

p. 96   "one day, some three weeks . . ." Otto Frisch, *What Little I Remember*, p. 176.

p. 96   "entered the room . . ." Peter Goodchild, *J. Robert Oppenheimer: Shatterer of Worlds*, p. 167.

p. 97   "Despite the best . . ." Herbert Feis, *The Atomic Bomb and the End of World War II*, p. 248.

8

THE INSIDER

With the end of the war, the men and women working at Los Alamos breathed a collective sigh of relief. Like almost all Americans, the scientists and technicians who had worked on the bomb yearned to return to normal life. For many, this meant leaving the rough desert town and going back to universities throughout America and Europe. Foremost among those wishing to change back to civilian life was Robert Oppenheimer.

Soon after the Japanese surrender, Oppenheimer informed General Groves of his intention to return to university life. Reluctantly, Groves accepted Oppenheimer's resignation, but before Oppenheimer left, Groves presented a certificate of appreciation from the army to the Los Alamos Laboratory in a ceremony on October 16, 1945. Accepting the award on behalf of the lab, Oppenheimer gave an eloquent speech that showed he had begun to grapple with the moral problem of the weapon that he helped to create:

> If atomic bombs are to be added to the arsenals of the world, or the arsenals of nations preparing for war, then the time will come when mankind will curse the name of Los Alamos and Hiroshima.
> The peoples of the world must unite or perish. This war, that has ravaged so much of the earth, has written these words. The atomic bomb has spelled them out for all men to understand.

This need for some sort of interlocking system of world governance to protect humankind from itself would guide Oppenheimer's understanding of world events for the rest of his life. He still had not renounced the acquisition of personal and political power for himself within the U.S. government (he was too driven a person to do that). But he would try to use whatever power came his way to control the potentially devastating force of atomic energy.

Oppenheimer was now more or less a free man, but he was no longer an obscure scientist. The enormous, even notorious, success of the atom bomb had transformed Robert Oppenheimer into a well-known and highly respected public figure. Oppenheimer derived tremendous personal and political clout from his fame, although he was not yet sure how or if he wanted to use it.

Within weeks after the awards ceremony at Los Alamos, Oppenheimer returned to California to take up a position on the faculty of the California Institute of Technology in Pasadena. Fitfully, he began to try to do basic physics research again, but his appetite for pure theory and research seemed to have waned during the war years. He did eventually publish a few papers about mesons, subatomic particles in the atomic nucleus that are even smaller than neutrons and protons.

Just before the war the Japanese physicist Hideki Yukawa had predicted the existence of mesons, but almost immediately research in these and other nuclear phenomena was dropped in favor of more practical wartime needs. The energies of most physicists had gone into projects such as the making of the atomic bomb that were as much about engineering as pure science. Now, after the war, many physicists returned to the eternal problem of the basic composition of the atom, of explaining what it was at its most elemental form. Happily for many physicists, this sort of research was not directly related to military work. Instead, it marked a return to the favorite work of theoretical physicists, the playful exploration of matter.

After the war, physicists no longer considered protons, neutrons and electrons to be elemental particles, the most basic building blocks of nature. Yukawa's prediction of the existence of the meson had changed all that. Now theoretical physicists concentrated their efforts on categorizing and explaining a bewildering array of subatomic particles—units that were given strange names, such as quarks and antiquarks, baryons, hadrons, gluons, leptons and the like—which seemed to constitute the bits and pieces of all matter.

As much as he tried, Oppenheimer could not find the time or motivation for this type of research. He published only four papers on theoretical physics after the war, none of them after 1950. Perhaps he slipped into the common thinking of the time that physicists were washed up after their 30th birthday, that a physicist's best work always came in his youth. In any event, the U.S. government beckoned Oppenheimer, soliciting his services again and again as a senior science adviser. It seems likely that Oppenheimer considered his work as a key player in U.S. nuclear policy to be more important that a return to work on theoretical research. Certainly his role as "father of the nuclear bomb" and science guru at-large to the government appealed to him because it was a spectacle played on a grander stage than the one offered him in academic life.

Oppenheimer's first reward for his wartime achievements came almost immediately after his move to Pasadena, when he was invited to testify on behalf of the May-Johnson bill, a piece of legislation whose purpose was to make the industrial and scientific apparatus of the Manhattan Project a permanent part of the American government. Oppenheimer spoke out strongly in favor of this bill, even though one of its key provisions allowed military officers to control America's nuclear machine.

Oppenheimer's testimony was greeted with dismay at Los Alamos, where many of the remaining scientists had lobbied vigorously for civilian administration and control of atomic research and uranium production. To many on the Hill, as Los Alamos was called by those who worked there, Oppenheimer had snuggled up too close to conservatives in the Congress and the War Department. Oppenheimer justified his actions by stating that the May-Johnson bill would encourage fast action toward international control of atomic weapons.

Early in 1946, the U.S. government again asked Oppenheimer's help, this time to participate on the U.S. team that would attempt to negotiate an international atomic arms treaty through the United Nations Atomic Energy Commission, a branch of the newly created United Nations. The international control of atomic weapons was one of Robert Oppenheimer's central concerns, and he was heartened by the response his suggestions received in Washington. With the help of Assistant Secretary of State Dean Acheson, Oppenheimer fashioned a negotiating position in which the

United States promised to give up its nuclear weapons and share nuclear information with other nations, particularly the Soviet Union, in exchange for an opening of the scientific laboratories and military factories of all nations to international inspection.

This idea, which Oppenheimer had borrowed from Niels Bohr, was seriously undermined when President Truman appointed the conservative investment banker Bernard Baruch to head the U.S. negotiating team. Baruch insisted that all decisions made by the U.N. commission be decided by majority vote, and that no nation be allowed a veto. The Soviet Union, which was at least as suspicious of the United States as the U.S. was of it, balked at the no-veto setup of the U.N. commission. Instead, the Soviets insisted they would not allow any U.N. inspection of their nuclear installations and demanded that the United States give up its nuclear arms before proceeding on further talks.

Despite the tough Soviet negotiating stance, Oppenheimer believed talks could move ahead if Baruch compromised on the idea of a majority vote in the U.N. committee. To protest Baruch's position, Oppenheimer met directly with President Truman. The meeting did not go well. At one point, Oppenheimer protested that he "had blood on his hands" because of his work in helping to build the bomb. Deeply offended by Oppenheimer's remark, Truman told an aide, "Don't bring that fellow around here again. After all, all he did was make the bomb. I'm the guy who fired it off." Baruch remained as head of the U.S. delegation; Oppenheimer eventually resigned; and the U.N. conference fell apart amid bickering and distrust between the United States and the Soviet Union.

Robert Oppenheimer's position as a government insider was hardly tarnished by this episode. Throughout 1946, he testified several times before Senate and House committees that were drafting legislation to replace the May-Johnson bill. Late in 1946 this latest bill, the Atomic Energy Act, passed both houses and was signed into law by President Truman. The law created a new federal agency, the Atomic Energy Commission (AEC), to handle all U.S. atomic matters. The AEC permanently replaced the Manhattan Project, and unlike the May-Johnson bill, stipulated civilian control for atomic power plants; the government factories in Oak

Ridge, Tennessee, and Hanford, Washington, that produced enriched uranium and plutonium; the Los Alamos Laboratory; and any other future plants or laboratories engaged in atomic weapons work.

The first Atomic Energy Commission was headed by David Lilienthal, an associate of Franklin Roosevelt's who formerly had been head of one of Roosevelt's New Deal creations, the Tennessee Valley Authority. As head of the Tennessee Valley Authority, Lilienthal had worked closely with Oppenheimer and General Groves to supply huge amounts of electricity to the Manhattan Project's uranium enrichment plants at Oak Ridge. During this time Oppenheimer and Lilienthal had become close friends. One of Lilienthal's first duties as commissioner of AEC was to appoint a General Advisory Board of scientists, and to no one's surprise his first appointment to this group was Robert Oppenheimer.

At the same time Oppenheimer was appointed to the AEC's General Advisory Board, he also won appointment as director of Princeton University's prestigious Institute for Advanced Study. Created in the 1920s, the institute had long been a haven for noted scientists and philosophers. At the time of Oppenheimer's appointment, Albert Einstein was probably the most famous scholar in residence at the institute. A position at the institute entailed no teaching work nor administrative duty (except for the director, whose administrative duties were light). The notables who landed there were required to do nothing more than pursue their thoughts amid the bucolic quiet of the New Jersey countryside. Oppenheimer had not always thought highly of the place. In the 1930s, perhaps because he was still something of an outsider and had not yet been invited to the institute as a fellow, he had dismissed it as "a madhouse, its . . . luminaries shining in separate and helpless desolation." By 1947, he had come to occupy a very different position relative to the power élite, and he found Princeton and its institute much to his liking.

As a result of these changes, Oppenheimer moved to Princeton in 1947 and began a work routine that required him to shuttle constantly between Princeton and Washington, D.C. Oppenheimer's appointment to the AEC's General Advisory Board would last until 1952 and probably gave him the greatest satisfac-

Albert Einstein and Robert Oppenheimer at the Institute for Advanced Study, Princeton, New Jersey, 1947. (Alfred Eisenstaedt, *Life* magazine © 1947 Time Warner Inc.)

tion of all the work he performed during this period. However, doubts about his loyalty to the United States still lingered in the halls of power in Washington. In March 1947, the FBI, which had taken charge of Oppenheimer's wartime security file from the army, passed along all of the old information that the army had gathered about Oppenheimer in the early years of the war, plus some new information, to David Lilienthal.

The contents of the FBI file surprised Lilienthal and the other commissioners. They had been completely unaware of Oppenheimer's "leftwandering," and in response to the FBI warning, Lilienthal and fellow AEC commissioner Lewis Strauss called a secret meeting of the commission to discuss whether or not the commission should keep Oppenheimer as an adviser and grant him a security clearance allowing him access to all U.S. atomic secrets.

Lilienthal and Strauss both were personal friends of Oppenheimer's, and Strauss had been instrumental in securing Oppenheimer the directorship of the Institute of Advanced Study. Accordingly, they were not disposed to believe the information the FBI had dumped into their laps. The commissioners approached those with whom Oppenheimer worked during the war.

General Advisory Committee of the Atomic Energy Commission, 1947. *Left to right:* **James Conant, Robert Oppenheimer, General James McCormack, Hartley Rowe, John Manley, I. I. Rabi, Roger Werner.** (Los Alamos National Laboratory)

Vannevar Bush and James Conant both testified strongly in favor of Oppenheimer, stating that he had "clearly demonstrated his loyalty" to his country during his tenure at Los Alamos. Even the FBI director, J. Edgar Hoover, eventually was forced to admit that the "investigation of Oppenheimer has been negative."

By the summer of 1947, the commissioners of the AEC had decided to keep Robert Oppenheimer as head of the General Advisory Counsel. The charges against him seemed too flimsy, and his service to his country too important to dismiss him from government service. Still, for at least one commissioner, Lewis Strauss, the FBI files had tarnished Oppenheimer's shining reputation. The files, coupled with a subtle but growing personality conflict between the two men, would eventually turn Strauss against Oppenheimer.

For now, though, Robert Oppenheimer stood at the pinnacle of his career. He was the driving force behind the reorganization of the U.S. nuclear effort. At his urging, vast sums were allocated to new nuclear science laboratories at Argonne, Illinois, and Brookhaven, New York. Los Alamos Laboratory was redone from top to bottom. The processing of plutonium was shifted to other sites, and Los Alamos was made into a lab for pure research. The reactors at Hanford were modernized, as were the facilities at Oak Ridge. Even though these efforts would appear to be at odds with his oft-stated desire for nuclear arms control, Oppenheimer justified his postwar work by insisting he had more power to influence events from the inside of government than as a protester on the outside. Privately, he admitted to many of his friends that he had given up hope for any meaningful nuclear arms treaty between the world's great powers.

During this period, Oppenheimer continued to dabble in theoretical physics. He organized an annual conference on high-energy physics at which top physicists from around the world gathered to discuss new ideas and approaches to understanding atomic structure. But he had now grown into something more than a humble scientist. His extraordinary dual position as scientist and public servant was acknowledged by the first issue in 1948 of the new American science journal *Physics Today*, which featured a photograph of a porkpie hat perched amid the pipes and valves of

Robert Oppenheimer's famous porkpie hat, from cover of *Physics Today*, 1948. (J. Robert Oppenheimer Memorial Committee)

a piece of heavy machinery. No caption was needed to explain the meaning of the photo: Everyone in American science and government knew the hat belonged to Robert Oppenheimer. The cover photo merely confirmed the obvious: more than any other single individual Robert Oppenheimer personified the glorious achievements of American science in the middle of the 20th century.

CHAPTER 8 NOTE

p. 99   "If atomic bombs . . ." Peter Goodchild, *J. Robert Oppenheimer: Shatterer of Worlds*, p. 172.

9

THE FALL

During the years immediately following World War II, Robert Oppenheimer discovered that despite his great personal status he was not above criticism. Some of the complaints aimed at him were the result of decisions he made as chairman of the AEC's General Advisory Committee; others were the result of his occasional awkward personality. The heady achievements during the war had revived a personality trait that had never completely left him—the arrogant and dismissive way he dealt with colleagues and equals that he termed "the beastliness." More than any other single reason, this character flaw would bring grief to Oppenheimer and set the stage for his tragic fall from power.

The first of his problems arose immediately after the war. At that time, Edward Teller and a small team of physicists at Los Alamos were still hard at work trying to perfect the bigger version of the atomic bomb they termed the Super. Yet, despite Teller's hard work, the project had not gone well. The basic idea behind the Super was that a huge increase in explosive power could be realized from an atomic bomb if a small amount of heavy hydrogen were attached to the nuclear weapon. Teller speculated that either deuterium (an isotope of hydrogen containing a proton and a neutron) or tritium (another hydrogen isotope containing one proton and two neutrons) could fuel the Super.

According to Teller's plan, the tremendous burst of heat emitted in the first split-second of an atomic explosion ought to fuse together atoms of deuterium or tritium, which would then release large amounts of energy. Unlike the fission process of uranium in the Fat Man or Little Boy atomic bombs, the fusing together of light tritium and deuterium atoms did not require a critical mass. Fusion required only intense heat (a temperature of about 400 million degrees Fahrenheit) supplied by the atomic bomb. These kinds of temperatures exist naturally only at the center of stars (fusion is the process that drives the release of energy from the Earth's sun) or in close proximity to a nuclear explosion, and the extent of release of energy derived from fusion is limited only by the amount of hydrogen, deuterium or tritium that is placed next to the source of this intense heat. Therefore, for a fusion bomb the only theoretical limit to the power released is the amount of tritium or deuterium placed inside the bomb next to the atomic weapon. The more tritium or deuterium that is placed inside the bomb and that can be successfully fused, the larger the explosion. It seemed possible, therefore, that a hydrogen bomb could be designed that would be hundreds, even thousands, of times more powerful than Fat Man or Little Boy.

This was how the Super was supposed to work. Unfortunately for Teller, the exact process for achieving this was difficult to figure out. Teller and his team could not even show mathematically that a process of sustained fusion would actually work in the split second before the energy from the fission bomb blew the deuterium and tritium apart.

Nonetheless, Teller maintained tenacious faith in the eventual success of his project, and around the time Oppenheimer left Los Alamos, Teller asked the lab's director to support him in his quest for the Super. Oppenheimer turned Teller down flat, and later, in his position as chairman of the AEC's General Advisory Committee, recommended that staff time and government money not be diverted to pursue fusion.

Oppenheimer's rejection hurt Teller deeply. First, it seemed to Teller that Oppenheimer was rejecting him personally, along with his competence and scientific ability. This feeling of personal rejection was made worse when Teller heard Oppenheimer say that the best scientists ought to leave the Los Alamos Laboratory. All the hard work had already been done, Oppenheimer implied, and anyone who remained behind was wasting his or her time.

Frustrated and discouraged, Teller did leave in 1946, and for several years took up a teaching position at the University of Chicago.

He had not given up on the Super, however, and by 1948 he would be back at Los Alamos, ready to take another stab at his pet project.

Oppenheimer apparently believed that the time of the scientists who remained at Los Alamos Laboratory would be better spent perfecting the still-crude fission bomb. By July 1947, the United States possessed only 13 nuclear weapons. With so small an arsenal of fission bombs, it seemed to Oppenheimer that the United States government would be better served by amassing a larger pile of proven weapons, rather than running off on the goose chase of fusion.

From a scientific and technical point of view, Oppenheimer's position made good sense to most of his fellow scientists. Politically, though, Oppenheimer was vulnerable to conservative critics who began to question why he was not more gung-ho in his pursuit of national defense. Coloring these arguments for and against a crash program to develop the hydrogen bomb was the rise of the Soviet Union as a world superpower.

After World War II, the Soviets brutally crushed democratic governments in the countries of eastern Europe controlled by their troops and replaced these governments with Communist dictatorships. Also, the Soviets made it clear that they supported Communist and leftist political organizations in many areas of the world that were still colonies of European powers such as England and France. This militant challenge to the United States and its allies alarmed many conservative politicians in the United States and set the stage for a political backlash against anyone or any group who had been associated with the Communist Party or with radical politics before the war. Mixed in with this hysterical reaction to the Soviet threat was the fear that the Soviets might be able to make an atomic bomb of their own.

Oppenheimer and other scientists associated with Los Alamos had briefed government leaders, including President Truman, about the likelihood of a Soviet bomb, concluding that it was impossible to stop the Soviets from acquiring the bomb. The only issue on which there was any debate at all was how long it would take the Soviets to come up with a nuclear weapon. At the end of World War II, American officials estimated that the Soviets would need seven to 10 years to accomplish this feat. This meant that the

United States would hold an unassailable monopoly on nuclear power probably until 1953 or 1954 at least.

Thus American officials were quite surprised when they, along with the rest of the world, learned that the Soviet Union had detonated its first nuclear weapon, code-named Joe I after Soviet dictator Josef Stalin, on September 23, 1949.

The first Soviet nuclear explosion frightened the American public and intensified the anti-Communist atmosphere within the United States. Many right-wing politicians especially began to foster the notion that the United States somehow had been betrayed by traitors from within, and congressional committees began inquiries into the political beliefs of ordinary and prominent Americans alike.

One of the most active of these congressional groups was the Un-American Activities Committee of the House of Representatives. The House Un-American Activities Committee (HUAC) had begun investigations into reputed Communist espionage activity in Ernest Lawrence's cyclotron laboratory in Berkeley in the days immediately prior to and during World War II. Because of his one-time close connections with several young physicists who had worked at Lawrence's lab, Oppenheimer was seen by HUAC members as a possible source of information about problems at the lab. Un-American Activities Committee investigators subpoenaed Oppenheimer to testify to the committee in 1949. The HUAC was also interested in Oppenheimer's brother Frank, who had recently been revealed as a longtime member of the Communist Party in a widely publicized newspaper article. During the war Frank Oppenheimer had worked at Oak Ridge and helped prepare the atomic test at Trinity, an arrangement that was sure to displease many HUAC members.

Oppenheimer's testimony began smoothly. The congressmen seemed somewhat awed by the physicist's reputation. One of the committee aides remarked that the HUAC was not "seeking to embarrass you [Oppenheimer]" and added that "your record of loyalty has been vouched for by General Groves." Committee members then proceeded to ask Oppenheimer about Rossi Lomanitz and other former students. Oppenheimer defended all of them, except one, Bernard Peters, whom Oppenheimer considered too radical to be trusted with secret government work. Oppenheimer's dismissal of Peters angered several of his friends and associates in Berkeley and elsewhere and marked a point of no return in Oppenheimer's relations with many he had known during his days of radical political activity in the 1930s.

Next, committee members asked Oppenheimer about his brother's Communist Party activities. At this point, Oppenheimer resorted to a courageous request. "Mr. Chairman," he said, "I ask you not to press these questions about my brother. If they are important to you, you can ask him. I will answer if asked, but I beg you not to ask me these questions." Remarkably, for a group that held the reputation of hounding and breaking the will of many witnesses appearing before it, every single congressman respected Robert Oppenheimer's request. Soon after, the committee adjourned, having satisfied itself with their interrogation of one of the nation's most respected scientists. Just before ending the session, many members of the committee, including a relatively obscure congressman from California named Richard Nixon, publicly praised Robert Oppenheimer. According to an Atomic Energy Commission lawyer who witnessed the session, Oppenheimer "charmed these congressmen out of their seats."

The following week, appearing before a different congressional committee and testifying about a technical matter, Robert Oppenheimer notched up another impressive public performance that at once demonstrated his great verbal skills and the withering sarcasm that earned him many enemies. This time Oppenheimer testified as an expert witness before the Joint Committee on Atomic Energy, a body composed of senators and congressmen that was investigating whether the Atomic Energy Commission had violated national security by shipping samples of radioactive isotopes to various scientific laboratories of some of America's allies. In particular, several senators and Commissioner Lewis Strauss of the AEC were concerned about a shipment of a radioactive isotope of iron that had been sent to a Norwegian defense plant to help trace the strength of steel in several casting techniques.

In Oppenheimer's opinion these isotopes had value only for the help they afforded scientists during routine scientific experiments. Further, he was adamant that these isotopes had no secret military value whatsoever. The isotopes, he said, "played no significant part" in the military use of atomic energy. Then aiming a barbed criticism at Lewis Strauss, the man who hired him as director of the Institute for Advanced Study and with whom he worked at the Atomic Energy Commission, he added: "You can use a shovel for atomic energy. In fact you do. . . . My own rating of the importance of isotopes . . . is that they are far less important than electronic devices, but far more important than, let us say, vitamins, somewhere in between." The committee room echoed with laughter after Oppenheimer's remarks, but significantly one member of the audience was not amused. According to a fellow AEC commissioner, Lewis Strauss carried "a look of hatred . . . that you don't see very often in a man's face." Strauss was not a man to forget slights. In time he would extract ample revenge on Robert Oppenheimer for Oppenheimer's clever but cruel treatment of him that day.

Oppenheimer's alienation of Lewis Strauss turned out to be a prelude to a much more serious test of wills between conservatives and liberals within the Truman administration. The successful test of Joe I, the first Soviet nuclear bomb, had put great pressure on the American government to respond in some way to the sudden insecurity felt by the American public. All during the fall of 1949, a fierce debate raged secretly between a number of government departments about what response the U.S. government should give to the Soviets. On one side, Edward Teller, Lewis Strauss and especially the U.S. Air Force demanded an immediate crash program to develop a workable hydrogen bomb. Arrayed against this group was a majority of the General Advisory Committee and for a time a majority of the commissioners of the AEC.

To Oppenheimer and many of his fellow scientists, the argument for immediate development of the hydrogen bomb exposed the need for a negotiated arms treaty. The call to arms issued by the generals and others marked for the scientists the beginning of a massive arms race whose course was littered with dangerous pitfalls. Other scientists on the General Advisory Committee noted that the hydrogen bomb was virtually useless as a military weapon; its explosive force was simply too huge to be used for anything but a war of total destruction. Even General Omar Bradley, the chief of staff of the army, noted that the H-bomb (as it had come to be called) had value mainly as a weapon of psychological terror. The H-bomb was destined to be a city destroyer, or as Oppenheimer wrote in an appendix of the General Advisory Committee report to the president, "a weapon of mass genocide." For this reason and because the technical problems involved in building the weapon still seemed so great, the General Advisory Committee voted against a crash program. Enrico Fermi, also a member of the General Advisory Committee, noted:

> *The fact that no limits exist to the destructiveness of this weapon makes its very existence and the knowledge of its construction a danger to humanity as a whole. It is necessarily an evil thing considered in any light. For these reasons, we believe it important for the President of the United States to tell the American public and the world that we think it is wrong on fundamental ethical principles to initiate the development of such a weapon.*

The military, the secretary of the newly named Department of Defense (formerly the War Department) and even the new secretary of state, Dean Acheson (formerly an ally of Oppenheimer), all disagreed with this assessment. If the United States could produce an H-bomb, these public officials reasoned, then the Soviets eventually would make their own, too. And the Soviet regime under the leadership of Josef Stalin would have no moral qualms whatsoever about constructing a weapon of mass destruction. Therefore, these officials urged President Truman to authorize the crash H-bomb program. On January 30, 1950, President Truman's press aide issued a statement from the president:

> *It is my responsibility as Commander-in-Chief of the Armed Forces to see to it that our country is able to defend itself against any possible aggressor. Accordingly, I have directed the Atomic Energy Commission to continue its work on all forms of atomic weapons, including the so-called hydrogen or super-bomb.*

In the same month that President Truman approved the crash H-bomb project, the British government discovered a spy in its atomic program. The offender's name was Klaus Fuchs. Fuchs was yet another German refugee physicist who had worked on the bomb at Los Alamos with the British team sent there during the war to help the Americans. This breach of security was disturbing enough; worse was the realization that Fuchs had been privy to most of Teller's H-bomb information as well.

Following quickly on the Fuchs scandal was an allegation, accusing Robert Oppenheimer of having been a member of the Communist Party, by a witness testifying before yet another Red-hunting committee, this one attached to the California state legislature. A Mrs. Sylvia Crouch, whose husband was a former Communist Party member in California, stated that Oppenheimer had hosted a "session of a top-drawer Communist group . . . a group so important that its makeup was kept secret from ordinary Communists."

Oppenheimer immediately issued a statement saying "that he had never been a member of the Communist Party" and had never hosted a Communist Party meeting "in my house or anywhere else." Mrs. Crouch's testimony, however, alerted the ever-vigilant FBI, which began renewed wiretaps and surveillance of the Oppenheimer family at Princeton and elsewhere. More ominously, rumors about Oppenheimer's loyalty began circulating throughout the government. Suspicions of Oppenheimer were especially pronounced among high air force officers and Lewis Strauss, who in 1952 had been appointed head of the Atomic Energy Commission after the retirement of Oppenheimer-ally David Lilienthal.

The air force distrusted Oppenheimer because it suspected him of standing in the way of the large role it sought for itself in the U.S. armed forces. The air force knew that a successful test of an H-bomb would translate into a gain for itself, because the air force would then be called on to develop airplanes and plans to deliver the gargantuan nuclear weapon in the event of war. In the simplest terms, a workable H-bomb meant a bigger and more important air force, a goal sought by every air force general.

Soon the air force began to make known its displeasure with Oppenheimer. The air force's chief scientist, David Griggs, stated to one of the AEC commissioners his view that "roadblocks [were] being put in the way [of the H-bomb] . . . that the General Advisory Committee, and specifically Dr. Oppenheimer had been interfering" with the project. Later, when Griggs confronted Oppenheimer directly with this accusation, Oppenheimer lashed out at him, accusing him of being "paranoid." Finally, in an attempt to mediate the dispute, the secretary of the air force, Thomas Finletter, invited Oppenheimer to lunch to discuss the problem. Oppenheimer's "beastliness" apparently was on full display during this encounter.

According to Finletter, the physicist's behavior had been "rude beyond belief." At the end of the meal, after Oppenheimer had left, Finletter told colleagues, "I don't feel you fellows have convinced me I should feel more positively about Dr. Oppenheimer."

By 1952, Oppenheimer's suggestions about national nuclear policy were being routinely ignored. Edward Teller and the mathematician Stanislaw Ulam had made a breakthrough in the design of the H-bomb that allowed the construction of a first crude hydrogen weapon. Rather than using simple heat to fuse the hydrogen atoms, Teller, at Ulam's suggestion, changed the bomb design to utilize heat from the tremendous burst of X rays emitted

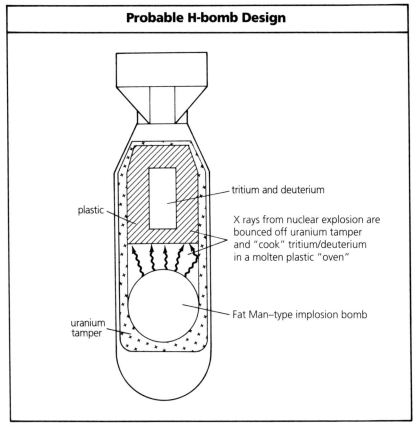

Probable H-bomb Design

tritium and deuterium

plastic

X rays from nuclear explosion are bounced off uranium tamper and "cook" tritium/deuterium in a molten plastic "oven"

Fat Man–type implosion bomb

uranium tamper

Figure 8

in the first milliseconds of an atomic bomb "trigger" explosion. These X rays, traveling at the speed of light (much faster than heat waves), effectively "cook" the hydrogen, providing the necessary heat for fusion before the shock waves from the atomic bomb "starter" blow the rest of the hydrogen weapon to bits.

The first test of this concept was held by the AEC on the island of Eniwetok in the South Pacific on November 1, 1952. Scientists expected the bomb, code-named Mike, to yield a blast of approximately 1 to 2 megatons, that is, about a hundred times more powerful than the 20-kiloton explosion at Hiroshima. Instead, the blast yielded 10.4 megatons, *500* times the Trinity and Hiroshima bomb. "The fireball expanded to 3 miles in diameter," one observer noted. Observers 40 miles away were almost overwhelmed by the force of the explosion. Scientists on the scene returned shaken and frightened by what they had unleashed. The bomb could not yet be delivered by an airplane (it weighed 65 tons and required a large refrigeration unit to cool the liquid tritium and deuterium that fueled the bomb). But the test represented a terrifying new chapter in the arms race.

Back in Washington, the whisper campaign against Oppenheimer intensified. Senator Joseph McCarthy, one of the most militant conservatives in Congress, had begun an investigation into Oppenheimer's Communist background. Also, the Joint Congressional Committee on Atomic Energy, the body before which Oppenheimer had so effectively ridiculed Lewis Strauss on an earlier occasion, had begun investigations into Oppenheimer's past. In December 1953, the Joint Committee sent a letter to the FBI and the AEC that categorically listed a series of damaging charges against Robert Oppenheimer. Among other things, it declared that Oppenheimer:

> between 1939 and 1942 was a sufficiently hardened Communist [who] either volunteered espionage information to the Soviets or complied with a request for such information . . .

> more probably than not has since [1942] been an espionage agent . . .

> more probably than not has since [1942] acted under a Soviet directive in influencing United States military, atomic energy, intelligence and diplomatic policies . . .

Alarmed at this new congressional investigation, one which also could tarnish the new image not only of Oppenheimer but of the Atomic Energy Commission, Lewis Strauss took action to cut off the Senate investigation before it began. Beginning at Christmas 1953, Strauss ordered that Oppenheimer not be informed of new U.S. atomic weapons developments. Further, the AEC began preparing charges against Oppenheimer along the lines of the Joint Committee accusations. If found guilty of these charges, which amounted to an accusation of treason, Oppenheimer would be stripped of his access to any U.S. nuclear secrets and forbidden to work in any capacity on the U.S. nuclear program.

Before proceeding against Oppenheimer, officials of the AEC quietly asked Oppenheimer to resign his position as chairman of the General Advisory Committee. When Oppenheimer refused to do this, Commissioner Strauss ordered the proceedings, which were secret, to begin.

The hearings ran from April 5 until May 6, 1954, and took the form of a trial. There were a few extraordinary differences between the proceedings against Oppenheimer and any other normal trial in any courtroom in the United States. First, all regular trials are public; the proceedings against Oppenheimer were secret until the *New York Times* found out about them and broke the news in mid-April. Second, in regular trials the defendant's lawyer has access to most, if not all, information available to prosecuting attorneys. In the Oppenheimer case, most of the information drawn against Oppenheimer was hidden from Oppenheimer's attorney, supposedly because of reasons of national security. Finally, much of the information used against Oppenheimer came from unnamed informants and illegal wiretaps. Both of these sources of information cannot be used in normal trials.

On June 28, 1954, the Atomic Energy Commission, whose very existence owed so much to the vision of the man now brought before it, voted to strip Robert Oppenheimer of his security clearance. In its final statement on the matter, the AEC judged that Robert Oppenheimer possessed "substantial defects of character and imprudent dangerous associations [with] known subversives" that made him unfit for continued government service.

Oppenheimer had not been found guilty of espionage. Rather, his main crime seems to have been his abrasive and arrogant personality and his resistance to the development of the H-bomb during the years 1945 to 1950 (when it seemed that a workable H-bomb was technically impossible). In any event, Oppenheimer's flirtation with power was over. The American government wouldn't be needing his advice and counsel anymore.

CHAPTER 9 NOTES

p. 113   "You can use a shovel . . ." *The New York Times*, June 16, 1949.

p. 114   "The fact that no limits . . ." Herbert York, *The Advisors*, p. 150.

p. 114   "It is my responsibility . . ." *The New York Times*, February 1, 1950.

p. 117   "Between 1939 and 1942 . . ." Philip Stern and Harold Green, *The Oppenheimer Case*, p. 219.

10

PICKING UP THE PIECES

As suddenly as it had come, the storm that demolished Robert Oppenheimer's life passed, and it its wake left a hollow quietness. Oppenheimer, who had grown to relish the power and prestige lavished upon him as a result of his high government service, now faced a difficult period of adjustment. To get away from the crush of reporters and ringing phones following the AEC's decision to banish him from government, Oppenheimer and his family took an extended holiday at their vacation house on the Virgin Islands (after the war, Oppenheimer had gradually given up Perro Caliente, his New Mexico ranch, in favor of the sea climate of the Caribbean).

They left behind them an American public still fearful of communism and of the Soviet Union. In this environment, any hint of disagreement with the views of right-wing politicians or whisper of impropriety quickly turned into attacks against an individual's loyalty and personal integrity. During his trip to the Virgin Islands, Oppenheimer again fell prey to these distorted fears. Somehow, the FBI picked up rumors, supposedly from agents inside the Soviet espionage network, that the Soviets were preparing to lure Oppenheimer to defect to the Soviet Union. Panicked FBI agents began to hunt for Oppenheimer. Once they knew where he was, they waited for his return to the United States to grill him at length about this rumor. Oppenheimer categorically denied these allegations and assured the FBI that he would immediately notify them if such an offer were ever made to him. Publicly, Oppenheimer reproached the FBI for its stupidity, saying, in the words of one FBI agent, that "while he [Oppenheimer] thought the Russians were . . . fools, he didn't think they were foolish enough to approach him with such an offer." Privately, Oppenheimer must have wondered if his torment would ever end.

While Oppenheimer was away in the Caribbean, Lewis Strauss, who had done so much to destroy Oppenheimer's government career, busied himself trying to finish off his former friend's academic respectability. Strauss, who had won Oppenheimer the job of director of the Institute for Advanced Study, now pushed Princeton University to fire Oppenheimer from that position. At one point during the summer, Strauss bragged to an associate that "if Oppenheimer would not submit his resignation, it would be requested" and that "of the 13 members of the Board of Trustees [of the Institute for Advanced Study], 8 of them would vote to oust Oppenheimer." But, apparently, most of the board, after having a few months to consider this demand more carefully, abandoned Strauss's vindictive course. In October 1954, Oppenheimer was reelected director. He was to remain at the institute for the rest of his life.

The first few years after the AEC trial were the roughest for Oppenheimer and his family. Both he and his wife Kitty began to drink more than was good for them. A number of friendships and associations were permanently severed, notably the Oppenheimers' close connection with Haakon Chevalier and his wife and Oppenheimer's professional relationship with Edward Teller. But a number of Oppenheimer's other colleagues lent him their emotional support, especially Hans Bethe, Niels Bohr and Robert Bacher, a physicist who had worked with Oppenheimer at Cal Tech and Los Alamos.

Oppenheimer busied himself with acquiring promising young physicists for the staff of the Institute for Advanced Study, and in doing so ran afoul of other members of the faculty, especially the mathematicians, who felt that he weighted the faculty too heavily in favor of physicists. Oppenheimer defended himself vigorously and was delighted when two of his proteges, T. D. Lee and C. D. Yang, won a Nobel Prize in physics in 1957.

For the most part, Oppenheimer accepted his downfall with grace, and the ordeal of the secret trial and its outcome seemed to mellow him. "I cannot sit with anger," he said to one interviewer in response to how he had managed to put his bitterness and disappointment behind him.

With so much time on his hands, Oppenheimer had more opportunity to be with his family, and he tried to engage more in fatherly activities with his daughter, Toni, and his son, Peter. He spent Sundays with his children and squeezed in some TV-watching time and card games with them, but these things did not come naturally to him. From a very early age, he had been taught that a certain formality comes with home life, and sitting down to watch television did not conform to his ideas of how free time should be spent. He loved his children and tried to show his affection to them, but his interests were demanding and difficult: French poetry, Indian philosophy, classical music. Unfortunately, these were not activities that teenagers readily understood or appreciated.

Oppenheimer had an especially difficult relationship with his son. He expected much of him, but Peter found it hard to follow in his father's footsteps. In 1958, when Peter failed an entrance exam into Princeton, Oppenheimer reacted with fury and refused to take Peter along with the family on an Easter trip to Europe. Later that spring, Peter dropped out of high school and, much like Oppenheimer himself at that age, went out West to think things over. He spent several months with Oppenheimer's brother, Frank. Frank, too, had suffered during the 1950s. He had been dismissed from his teaching job at the University of Minnesota after his former ties to the Communist Party became public. Unable to find another job in teaching or research of physics, Frank bought a sheep ranch in Colorado and settled down to a quiet life, but one on which his training and intellect were wasted.

The anticommunist hysteria of the 1950s, sometime called McCarthyism, after Senator Joseph McCarthy of Wisconsin, one of the major players in the communist witchhunt, claimed quite a few careers besides Frank Oppenheimer's. Robert Oppenheimer's former students David Bohm, Rossi Lomanitz and Bernard Peters all were hounded by the FBI and U.S. State Department in the decade following the end of World War II.

Bohm, who had followed Oppenheimer to Princeton, was tried and acquitted of contempt of Congress in 1949, after refusing to testify about his past before the House Un-American Activities Committee. Dismissed from his teaching post at Princeton, Bohm left the United States for the University of Sao Paulo in Brazil, the only faculty that had offered him a job. Later he managed with some difficulty (because his passport was seized by U.S. embassy officials in Brazil) to travel to England to teach.

Rossi Lomanitz, who had spent the war years as a private in the army because of fears about his loyalty on the part of U.S. Army counterintelligence, managed to secure a job teaching physics at Fisk University after the war. Lomanitz, too, was eventually summoned to testify about his past before the HUAC, and he also invoked the Fifth Amendment (which protects a person from testifying against him- or herself) and refused to cooperate. Because of this, he was fired from Fisk, and throughout the 1950s held a series of manual labor jobs in Oklahoma. Finally, in the early 1960s, he got a job from an old Berkeley friend as a consulting physicist for the General Electric Company. In the mid-1960s he returned to academic life, teaching physics at the New Mexico Institute of Mining Technology, a small college in Socorro, New Mexico.

Even after his return to full-time academic life in 1954, Oppenheimer steered clear of people like Bohm and Lomanitz. Oppenheimer viewed these former students, who had so idolized him in Berkeley in the 1930s, as sources of trouble. He wanted nothing more to do with those times. They had ruined him utterly, and he ruthlessly cut out of his life all of his radical comrades from that era.

It is interesting to note that near the end of his life, in 1964, Oppenheimer received a letter from one of these people, his former colleague at Berkeley, Haakon Chevalier. Chevalier, who was writing a book about Oppenheimer and the scene at Berkeley before World War II, asked for Oppenheimer's permission to go public with information that Chevalier had been holding since the early 1940s. "The reason for my writing you," Chevalier said,

> *is that an important part of [my] story concerns your and my member-*
> *ship in the same unit of the CP [Communist Party] from 1938 to 1942.*
> *I should like to deal with this in its proper perspective, telling the facts*
> *as I remember them. As this is one of the things in your life which, in*
> *my opinion, you have least to be ashamed of . . . I consider it a grave*
> *omission not to give it its due prominence.*

Oppenheimer sent Chevalier back a stilted reply: "I have never been a member of the Communist Party, and thus have never been a member of a Communist Party Unit. I, of course, have always known this. I thought you did too." Honoring Oppenheimer's request, Chevalier said nothing about Oppenheimer's relationship with the party in his book. Nevertheless, several tantalizing questions remain: Was Oppenheimer a member of the Communist Party? And, if so, did he spy for the party and the Soviet Union? Based on Chevalier's private letter to Oppenheimer, the answer to the former question seems to be "yes." To the latter question, no answer can be given, although it is well to remember that membership in the party during a time of grave economic problems and personal soul-searching does not necessarily translate into espionage against one's own country.

By the late 1960s, Oppenheimer had become something of a free-lance expert on the problems of war, nuclear arms and arms

Kitty and Robert Oppenheimer in Osaka, Japan, 1960, with Mr. and Mrs. Kiyokata Kusaka of the Japanese Committee for Intellectual Exchange. (J. Robert Oppenheimer Memorial Committee)

President Lyndon Johnson presenting the AEC's Fermi Award to Oppenheimer in December 1963. (J. Robert Oppenheimer Memorial Committee)

control. He met often with visiting foreign dignitaries and arranged seminars to discuss how to resolve conflicts peacefully rather than by war. In 1960, in a personal peace-making pilgrimage of his own, Oppenheimer traveled to Japan to attend a meeting of the Japanese Committee for Intellectual Exchange.

By the early 1960s, the hostility exhibited by the U.S. nuclear establishment toward Oppenheimer had begun to wane. McCarthyism had died out at the end of the 1950s, and a new, more tolerant era was ushered in with the election in 1960 of John Kennedy as president. In 1963, the General Advisory Committee of the Atomic Energy Commission voted to award its Enrico Fermi Award for excellence in the field of nuclear research to Oppenheimer. This gesture of reconciliation was engineered by Edward Teller, who had received the Fermi Award in 1962.

Even though Teller had spoken against Oppenheimer during the secret AEC hearings in 1954, he obviously felt bad about Oppenheimer's treatment in the ensuing years and sought some way to make amends for the very hard feelings resulting from this episode. The award, a symbolic act of forgiveness and acceptance on the part of the government, was to be presented by the president in a formal ceremony at the White House. Two weeks before the award ceremony, on November 22, 1963, President Kennedy was assassinated in Dallas, Texas. Lyndon Johnson, the new president, presented the prize to Oppenheimer on December 2. Blinking back tears, Oppenheimer responded to a gracious speech by Johnson, which thanked him for his contributions to the nation's well-being in the peaceful as well as military use of atomic energy. "I think it is just possible, Mr. President, that it has taken some charity and some courage for you to make this award today. That would seem to me a good augury for all our futures."

In 1966, Robert Oppenheimer was diagnosed as suffering from cancer of the throat. Unable to continue his duties at the Institute for Advanced Study, he gave up the directorship. Throughout the year, he received radiation therapy against the cancer, but by the fall it was apparent he was losing the battle. On February 18, 1967, he died at his home in Princeton. He was 62 years old.

A fitting epitaph for his life can be found in the words of a speech he gave at Los Alamos on a visit there after the war. "It is not possible," he said

> to be a scientist unless you believe that the knowledge of the world, and the power which this gives, is a thing which is of intrinsic value to humanity, and that you are using it to help in the spread of knowledge, and are willing to take the consequences.

CHAPTER 10 NOTES

p. 123 "is that an important part . . ." Peter Goodchild, *J. Robert Oppenheimer: Shatterer of Worlds*, p. 206.

p. 126 "It is not possible . . ." Alice Kimball Smith and Charles Weiner, eds., *Robert Oppenheimer: Letters and Recollections*, p. 315.

11

EPILOGUE: THE LEGACY OF ROBERT OPPENHEIMER

Robert Oppenheimer's turbulent life illustrates the challenges and dilemmas of the scientist in the 20th century. Oppenheimer brought a zest and irrepressible curiosity to his quest for truth, which is after all the essential goal of science. Along the way, Oppenheimer accomplished remarkable achievements in four broad areas: as a scientific administrator (shown remarkably at Los Alamos during the war, and in Washington until 1954); as an educator (particularly in Berkeley during the 1930s); as a theoretical physicist and synthesizer of ideas; and as a nuclear policymaker and advocate of international arms control. Any of these four achievements would be enough to make an individual scientist proud; together, they set a shining example for the generations of scientists who have followed Oppenheimer. Arguably, of all these efforts, Oppenheimer's most remarkable legacy is his courageous and visionary stand on the need for international arms control.

In 1963, nine years after Oppenheimer was forced out of government and 17 years after the failure of the first United Nations attempt at arms control, the United States and Soviet Union finally signed a nuclear arms control treaty. In this agreement, called the Limited Test Ban Treaty, both countries promised not to test nuclear weapons in the Earth's atmosphere, in space or in the oceans. Instead, the treaty limited nuclear weapons testing to underground sites so that radioactive fallout from these explosions would not pollute the Earth's environment. Furthermore, both countries called on other nations to sign the treaty as a first step in an international movement to limit the spread and testing of all nuclear weapons. This appeal worked; by 1990, 111 countries had signed the Limited Test Ban Treaty.

Even though it did nothing to actually reduce the number of nuclear weapons in the hands of the world's two superpowers— the United States and the U.S.S.R.—the Limited Test Ban Treaty represented an important first step on the road to international control of nuclear weapons. For almost 30 years now, since that first treaty in 1963, the United States and Soviet Union have continued their efforts to control the production and spread of nuclear weapons. This had been an up and down process in which each side has had to offer gestures of compromise and concession to gain the trust of the other.

A second important treaty came in 1968, when both countries signed the Non-Proliferation Treaty, whose goal was to prevent the acquisition of weapons by countries that did not possess them. In 1968, only five countries—the United States, Soviet Union, Britain, France and China—had developed nuclear weapons. All of these nuclear powers, except China, agreed to sign the Non-Proliferation Treaty, and more important, 124 nonnuclear countries also signed. In exchange for renouncing nuclear weapons, these non-nuclear countries were promised aid by the nuclear powers in developing the peaceful use of nuclear energy through the construction of nuclear-powered electrical-generation power plants. These types of power programs have proved to be helpful for many poor and developing nations because they provide a relatively cheap and reliable source of electricity for the industries and cities of these poorer countries. Since 1968, however, four other countries—Israel, Pakistan, India and South Africa—have probably added nuclear weapons to their military arsenals, a worrisome trend but one predicted as far back as 1942 by Niels Bohr and Robert Oppenheimer.

Beginning in 1972, the Soviet Union and United States began to tackle the more difficult problem of trying to limit, then reduce their stockpile of nuclear weapons, an inventory that included approximately 15,000 weapons on each side. In that year, the two countries signed the Strategic Arms Limitation Treaty (called after its initials "SALT"), which placed a limit on the number of long-range ground and seaborne missiles each side could possess. Even though the SALT agreement did not actually reduce the number of nuclear weapons on each side, it put a brake for the first time on the costly and dangerous arms race between the United States and the Soviet Union that had existed since the end of World War II. Other arms treaties, some of which had more success than others, followed the SALT agreement. A breakthrough agreement between both governments came only in 1989, with the first agreement in which both sides actually promised to reduce the number of nuclear weapons in their arsenals.

The spirit of Robert Oppenheimer at his best and most generous has guided these efforts. These treaties serve as an important reaffirmation of Oppenheimer's vision of a world in which conflict can be resolved by international negotiation rather than war. It was for this sort of world, one in which humankind is linked in a struggle for peace and mutual understanding, that Robert Oppenheimer worked and suffered throughout his life. And it is to all of us that he has left this unfinished business.

GLOSSARY

alpha particle: a helium nucleus, composed of two protons and two neutrons, emitted by a larger nucleus during radioactive decay.

atom: concept introduced by Democritus in 5th century B.C. Now conceived as the smallest chemical part of an element, but one that also is composed of subatomic particles such as quarks.

atomic bomb (or *fission bomb*): a military weapon whose explosive force is derived from the fissioning, or splitting apart, at enormous speeds of the elements uranium or plutonium.

atomic particles: until the 1940s, the basic component parts of the atom, including the neutron, proton, electron and positron. Since then, many of these units are understood to be composed of even smaller subatomic particles.

atomic spectrum: a unique band of lines produced by the atoms of every element when light emitted by that element is passed through a prism. These identify the element and show the energy levels of the atom's electrons as they pass from steady state to more excited states during heating.

beta particle: an electron or positron ejected from orbit of an atomic nucleus during radioactive decay.

binding energy: the amount of energy, expressed in volts of electricity, necessary to hold the nucleus of an atom together. Some of this energy is released when atoms fission or fuse.

chain reaction: a continuous and self-sustaining process of nuclear fission that occurs as a result of the accumulation of a critical mass of radioactive material such as uranium or plutonium.

cosmic rays: high-energy particles that pass into the Earth's atmosphere from space. These consist mostly of protons, but also include electrons, positrons, gamma rays and other forms of radiation.

critical mass: an exact amount of a radioactive substance, such as uranium and plutonium, needed to cause a chain reaction.

cyclotron: a machine that accelerates particles (neutrons, protons, electrons or atoms of elements such as uranium) by electrical magnetism through a circular track. Cyclotrons have been used to bombard atoms, breaking them apart so that subatomic particles can be observed, and to separate U-235 from U-238.

deuterium: an isotope of hydrogen containing one proton and one neutron (normal hydrogen has only one proton).

electron: a light, negatively charged particle found in orbit around the nucleus of an atom.

fission: a process whereby the nucleus of an atom (usually a heavy, unstable one such as uranium) splits, releasing binding energy and forming several different and lighter elements from the remains of the original nucleus.

fusion: the merging of two light atomic nuclei to form a single heavier atom (for instance, the fusion of tritium and deuterium to form helium).

gamma radiation: an almost weightless, fast, high-energy ray emitted by atomic nuclei passing to a lower energy state.

half-life: the amount of time during which an unstable, radioactive element such as uranium loses half its mass.

hydrogen bomb: a weapon consisting of a uranium or plutonium fission "trigger" bomb, which supplies a tremendous burst of heat that causes tritium and deuterium (two isotopes of hydrogen) to fuse into helium, releasing huge amounts of binding energy.

implosion: an inward compression of a substance, caused in the case of a nuclear weapon by a series of simultaneously fired explosives aimed inward toward a plutonium sphere.

isotopes: atoms of the same element (having the same number of protons) that possess different atomic properties owing to a different number of neutrons. For instance, U-235 fissions much more readily than U-238 because it has three less neutrons.

mass number: the total of protons and neutrons of an element or isotope.

neutron: a relatively heavy particle of neutral charge with a mass approximately equal to a proton. One of the two main particles making up the nucleus.

plutonium: element number 94, which does not occur naturally on Earth. First created and named by American chemist Glenn Seabory in 1940.

positron: a positively charged electron. The reverse image of an electron, called its antiparticle because the two annihilate each other when they come into contact.

proton: a relatively heavy particle possessing a positive electrical charge. One of the two main particles making up the nucleus.

quantum: a packet of energy, the minimum amount necessary for a system, such as the orbit of an electron around a nucleus, to change (for instance, to jump from one orbit level to another).

quantum mechanics theory: a theoretical system using the ideas of probability and quanta energy to explain how the atom functions and is held together.

quark: a subatomic particle from which protons and neutrons are created. Quarks carry a fractional electrical charge (unlike protons or electrons, which possess a whole positive or negative charge each, respectively) and are divided into different types: up, down, strange, charmed, bottom, top. The concept was proposed by American physicist Murray Gell-Mann in 1963 as a means to explain the electromagnetic forces that hold the atom together.

radioactivity: the spontaneous disintegration of some heavy atomic nuclei (such as uranium or radium) by the emission of neutrons, alpha particles, beta particles or gamma rays.

spectogram: a photograph of the visual line spectrum of an element, obtained when the light emitted by that element is passed through a prism and is broken into a unique series of bands.

tritium: an isotope of hydrogen possessing one proton and two neutrons.

uranium: a radioactive element, number 92 (possessing 92 protons), discovered in 1789. Uranium comes in several isotopes, the best known of which are U-235 and U-238. Uranium 238 accounts for more than 99% of all naturally occurring uranium; U-235 makes up just .7%. Uranium 235, however, is much more likely to fission that U-238 is and therefore valued for its use in nuclear power reactors and atomic weapons.

vacuum tube: a glass tube from which most, if not all gases, have been pumped, thereby creating a virtually empty space, one free of almost all atoms.

X ray: high-energy electromagnetic radiation, similar to gamma radiation, that is produced when atoms in a metal target are bombarded by electrons.

FURTHER READING

Books by Robert Oppenheimer

Oppenheimer, Robert. *Science and the Common Understanding.* New York: Simon & Schuster, 1954. Expressed in Oppenheimer's unique combination of elegant, nontechnical language, this book offers a firsthand look at physics, quantum mechanics and the role of the scientist in modern society.

———. *The Open Mind.* New York: Simon & Schuster, 1955. A collection of lectures given by Oppenheimer between the years 1946 and 1954, this book deals with the problems of atomic weapons and the relationship of science with the rest of society.

About Robert Oppenheimer

Chevalier, Haakon. *Oppenheimer: The Story of a Friendship.* New York: Braziller, 1965. An eloquent account of the friendship between Oppenheimer and Haakon Chevalier, including interesting sections about Communist Party activity in California during the 1930s.

Goodchild, Peter. *J. Robert Oppenheimer: Shatterer of Worlds.* New York: Fromm International, 1985. A full-length biography of Oppenheimer, and also the text accompanying PBS's documentary of Oppenheimer's life.

Michelmore, Peter. *The Swift Years: The Robert Oppenheimer Story.* New York: Dodd, Mead, 1969. A comprehensive, full-length look at the life of Robert Oppenheimer.

Rabi, I. I., Robert Serber, Victor Weisskopf, Abraham Pais, and Glenn Seaborg. *Oppenheimer.* New York: Charles Scribner's Sons, 1969. Oppenheimer's life as seen from five different angles; interesting in illuminating the different sides of a complex personality.

Smith, Alice, and Charles Weiner. *Robert Oppenheimer: Letters and Recollections.* Cambridge, Harvard University Press, 1980. Oppenheimer's life as revealed through his letters to close friends and colleagues, with brief but penetrating commentary.

Stern, Phillip (with Harold Green). *The Oppenheimer Case: Security on Trial.* New York: Harper & Row, 1969. Offers an in-depth look at the complicated dynamics surrounding Oppenheimer's problems with the U.S. government and Atomic Energy Commission.

U.S. Atomic Energy Commission. *In the Matter of J. Robert Oppenheimer, Transcript of Hearing Before Personnel Security Board and Texts of Principal Documents and Letters.* Cambridge, Mass.: MIT Press, 1971. The full transcript of the hearings that resulted in the removal of Oppenheimer's security clearance and fall from power within the government.

About Science, Scientists and Nuclear Physics

Davis, Nuel Pharr. *Lawrence and Oppenheimer.* New York: Simon & Schuster, 1968. An interesting examination of the relationship between two giants of American science.

Feyerabend, Paul. *Against Method.* London: Verson, 1975. A thought-provoking and critical examination of the role of science in modern society.

Guillemin, Victor. *The Story of Quantum Mechanics.* New York: Charles Scribner's Sons, 1968. An examination of the 30 or so fascinating years in which the theories of atomic physics were thoroughly revolutionized.

Kevles, Daniel. *The Physicists.* New York: Alfred A. Knopf, 1978. An interesting study of the evolution of physics in the United States from 1865 to the present.

Kuhn, Thomas. *The Structure of Scientific Revolution.* Chicago: University of Chicago Press, 1962. A ground-breaking book that probes how scientific discovery is made.

Segre, Emilio. *From X-Rays to Quarks.* San Francisco: W. H. Freeman, 1980. A fairly nontechnical account of the breakthroughs in physics from the middle of the 19th century to the present day.

Whitehead, Alfred. *Science and the Modern World.* New York: Free Press, 1925. One of the first modern examinations of the history and evolution of science, a classic masterpiece.

About Los Alamos and the Manhattan Project

Goudsmit, Samuel. *Alsos.* New York: Henry Schuman, 1947. A spirited account of the Alsos Mission, which uncovered the extent of German atomic research inside war-wracked Europe.

Groves, Leslie. *Now It Can Be Told: The Story of the Manhattan Project.* New York: Harper & Row, 1962. An insider's story of the development of the atomic bomb by the U.S. government.

Lamont, Lansing. *Day of Trinity.* New York: Atheneum, 1965. An account of the work at Los Alamos during the war.

Rhodes, Richard. *The Making of the Atomic Bomb.* New York: Simon & Schuster, 1986. A masterful and comprehensive retelling of the relationships between science, government and society that resulted in the creation of the atomic bomb.

About the Bombing of Hiroshima

Hachiya, Michihiko. *Hiroshima Diary.* Chapel Hill, N.C.: University of North Carolina Press, 1955; and Ibuse, Masuji. *Black Rain.* New York: Kodansha International, 1969. Two chilling and unblinking looks at the result of atomic warfare.

INDEX
Italic numbers indicate illustrations